LEADERS

OF THE
MIDDLE
EAST

James
Haskins

ENSLOW PUBLISHERS, INC.

Bloy St. & Ramsey Ave.   P.O. Box 38
Box 777   Aldershot
Hillside, N.J. 07205   Hants GU12 6BP
U.S.A.   U.K.

Library of Congress Cataloging in Publication Data

Haskins, James, 1941-
    Leaders of the Middle East.

    Bibliography: p.
    Includes index.
    Summary: Presents biographical information on nine men
who have been in leadership positions in the Middle Eastern
countries.
    1. Near East—Kings and rulers—Biography—Juvenile liter-
ature. [1. Heads of state. 2. Kings, queens, rulers, etc.
3. Near East—History] I. Title.
DS61.5.H37   1985   956'.009'92 [B] [920]   84-6150
ISBN 0-89490-086-2

Printed in the United States of America

10 9 8 7 6 5 4 3 2

Illustration Credits
Compliments of Consulate General of Israel in New York,
p. 62; Courtesy of Jordan Mission to the United Nations,
p. 96; Courtesy of Pakistan Embassy, Washington, D.C.,
p. 156; Compliments of the Permanent Mission of the Syrian
Arab Republic to the United Nations, p. 48; Courtesy of
Saudi Arabia Embassy, Washington, D.C., p. 80; Compliments
of the State Information Service, p. 126; United Press International Photos, pp. 30, 110, 140.

Contents

ACKNOWLEDGEMENTS

I am grateful to Patricia McKissack for her help with this book. Thanks are due also to Kathy Benson, Elza Dinwiddie, and the various Missions to the United Nations that provided photographs and other materials.

J.H.

FOREWORD

In the seemingly unending chaos of Middle Eastern politics, leaders often rise suddenly to prominence in newspaper reports and then disappear again, much like Shakespeare's "poor player that struts and frets his hour upon the stage and then is heard no more." Who are the men who control events in that war-torn part of the world? What influences shaped their characters?

This book tells the story of Middle Eastern history and recent politics through the biographies of some of the region's major leaders. It gives the reader a chance to get beneath the newspaper headlines and as such is valuable background reading for anyone with an interest in what is happening in the Middle East.

Richard W. Bulliet

Professor of History
Director, Middle East
Institute
Columbia University

1

What Is
the Middle East
and Why
Is It Important?

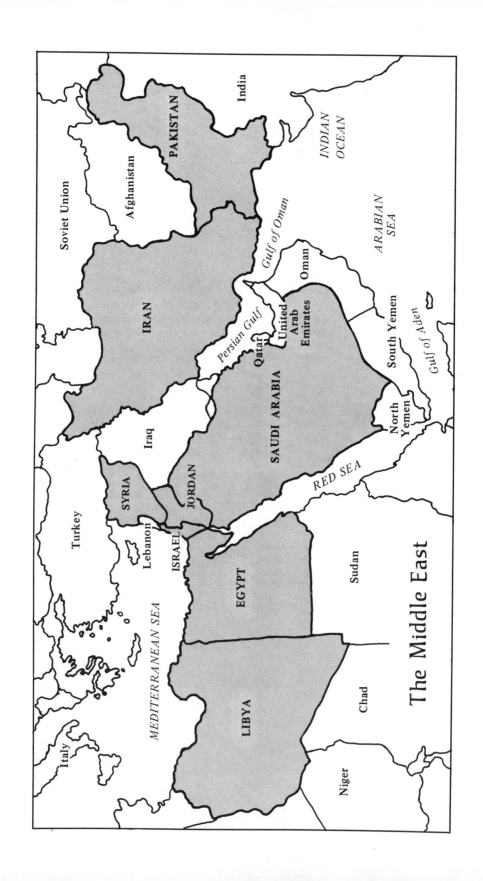

The Middle East

1

~~~~~~

If you try to find the Middle East on a map, you will not find any area labelled with the words "Middle East." It is not a continent, like Africa or Asia. While most of the countries are in the area at the eastern end of the Mediterranean Sea, the region also includes countries in southwest Asia and northeast Africa. What defines the Middle East more than geography is its culture, which includes its religions and its languages. As we shall see, however, even culturally, the Middle East is hard to define.

The term Middle East came into use during World War II, when the British military command in Egypt was given the title "Middle East Command." At that time, the term was used to cover the military theater, which was made up of the territory that now includes the states of Turkey, Greece, Cyprus, Syria, Lebanon, Iraq, Iran, Israel, Jordan, Egypt, the Sudan, Libya, and the various states of the Arab Peninsula. Over the past forty years, the definition has changed from a military one to one based more on culture. (Today Greece and Cyprus are not considered part of the Middle East.)

Now there are really two ways to define the Middle East. By one definition, the area includes the Asian part of Turkey, and Syria, Israel, Jordan, Iran, Iraq, Lebanon, Saudi Arabia, Yemen,

Southern Yemen, Oman, the United Arab Emirates, Qatar, Bahrain, Kuwait, Egypt, and Libya. By the second definition, the Middle East also includes eastern Mediterranean countries that are predominantly Islamic in culture. Thus, in addition to the countries listed above it includes the remaining states of North Africa as well as Afghanistan and Pakistan. The second, broader definition is used in this book.

Although there may be differences of opinion about how to define the Middle East, there is no problem in defining the area as one of the most troubled in the world today. The Middle East has been in turmoil for many years and the prospects for peace in the area are still dim. The reasons for the continued unrest in the Middle East are varied and complex. Some sources of conflict are centuries old, while others date back only a few decades or a few years. They include religious, political, and economic divisions, and many combinations of all three. One key to understanding the problems in the Middle East today is the fact that it is a conglomeration of states with very diverse interests. This is true despite the fact that, on the surface at least, most of these states seem to have much in common.

The vast majority of the people in the Middle East are Moslems. Their religion, which is called Islam, was founded by the Prophet Mohammed in the seventh century A.D. Mohammed believed he was selected by God as the last of the prophets and as the successor of Jesus Christ. He believed that his mission was to bring the word to his fellow Arabs—and all the other people of the earth—that there is only one God and that man must submit to Him in all things. Islam, an Arabic word, means "submission to, or having peace with, God." The Islamic name for God is Allah.

Islam is a very strong religion and one of the most widespread in the world today. During his lifetime, Mohammed was remarkably successful in uniting the people of Arabia under Islam and persuading them to forsake their devotion to many different gods. He was not successful in converting many of the Christians and Jews in the Arab lands, even though he believed that Islam was a further development of Christianity and Judaism. After his death, his followers expanded the influence of Islam and organized its beliefs and practices.

The Koran, the most sacred book of Islam, was not actually published until twenty years after Mohammed's death. According to Islamic belief, it contains the revelations that God gave Mohammed during the course of his life. These revelations were written down by the Prophet's secretary and later edited and arranged under Uthman, Mohammed's third successor. Written in Arabic, the Koran is read in that language by all Moslems, no matter what their native tongue. Next in importance among Islamic writings is the Sunna, which is the way, or example, of the Prophet. Compiled some 200 years after the Prophet's death, it is really six collections of Mohammed's moral sayings and anecdotes about him and is an elaboration of the basic teachings of the Koran.

There are five duties that all Moslems must perform. One is to say at least once, with full understanding and absolute acceptance, "There is no God but Allah and Mohammed is his prophet." The second duty is to pray five times daily, each time facing Mecca, Mohammed's birthplace, which is located in what is now Saudi Arabia. The third is to give generously to the poor. The fourth is to fast (go without food) in the daylight hours during Ramadan, the ninth month of the Moslem year and the time when Mohammed received the first revelation of the Koran. The fifth duty is to make at least one pilgrimage to Mecca.

In addition to these five duties, there are many strict rules of Islam that true believers must obey and that govern their everyday lives. They must not eat pork, drink alcohol, or gamble. Women must be completely subservient to men—until very recently women enjoyed few legal rights and were supposed to keep their heads and faces covered at all times. In the last decade or so, some of these rules have been relaxed in some Islamic countries that have been exposed to Western ideas. In some countries it is not unusual to see Moslem men drinking or Moslem women without veils. The relaxation of some of these restrictions is one source of conflict in the Middle East: Islamic fundamentalists, who want to keep the old traditions, see Western values and ideas as a threat to their way of life.

There are many sources of conflict within Islam. The most serious split occurred in the early centuries of the faith and divided Moslems into two groups—Sunnis and Shiites. There was a disagreement over the caliphate, or leadership, of Islam. After Mohammed died his followers chose a caliph, or viceregent, of Allah. Ali, Mohammed's son-in-law and one of his most faithful followers, had expected to become caliph, but the position went to Abu Bakr instead. Ali was denied the caliphate two more times before he finally succeeded to that position. Still bitterly opposed by many influential Moslems, he was murdered. He was succeeded by his son Hasan, who was forced to abdicate by an opposition leader named Muawiya. Supporters of Muawiya—and their descendants—came to be called Sunni Moslems. Those who believed that the caliphate belonged in Mohammed's family, that Ali should have been the first caliph, and that on his death the caliphate should have passed to his descendants, came to be called Shiite Moslems.

Over the next centuries, there were sometimes two or three different caliphs at the same time, and after 1258 the caliphate practically ceased to exist. In 1517 when the Ottoman Turks captured Egypt, their Sultan took the title of caliph, but it was abolished in 1924. Since then, several pan-Islamic conferences have discussed reestablishing a caliphate, but the various Moslem states and sects have been unable to come to any agreement on the matter.

While the cause of the split in Islam became less important over the years, the two major Moslem sects kept moving further apart. The Sunnis view all other sects as erroneous. They have remained true to the original principles of Islam and consider themselves the orthodox of Islam. Today, eighty-five percent of all Moslems are Sunnis. In the middle 1700's Mohammed ibn Abd *al-Wahhab began a reform movement to restore Islam to its original purity by stripping it of all beliefs and practices that had been added after 950 A.D. The Wahhabi sect is strongest on the Arabian peninsula. Among its members are the ruling family of Saudi Arabia.

The Shiites have come to differ from the Sunnis in matters of law and ceremony. The Shiites remain strongest in Iran, but there are important Shiite communities in Iraq, Yemen, Pakistan, and Lebanon. And their influence is growing throughout the

---

*It is useful to know in dealing with Arabic names that *al-* and *el-* are translated as *the*.

region. More zealous and more nationalistic than the Sunnis, the Shiites have split into many different sects, including the Assassins, the Druses, the Fatimids, and the Ismailis.

Thus, while most of the people in the Middle East are Moslems, they differ greatly in the way they practice their religion and in their political beliefs. It is important to remember, too, that Islam is by no means the only important religion in the Middle East. In fact, both Judaism and Christianity had their origins in the Middle East, in the area called Palestine. There are Arab Christians and there are Arab Jews, but all except one Middle Eastern country have Islam as either the official or semiofficial religion.

Israel is the only non-Moslem country in the Middle East. Its official religion is Judaism. It is located in the area that is called Palestine and that is also called the Holy Land—by Jews because they believe God promised it to them, by Christians, because Jesus spent his life there, and by Moslems, because legend says the Prophet Mohammed ascended from Jerusalem on a visit to heaven.

Much of the unrest in the Middle East is due to the presence of the state of Israel, which was formed in 1947 from parts of Palestine. Under a United Nations order, Palestine was partitioned into an Arab state and a Jewish state. The Arabs who lived in Palestine refused to accept the UN order and wound up with no state at all. For nearly forty years, millions of Palestinians have been without a homeland. Some have settled and made new lives in other countries, but many live in refugee camps in neighboring states. Nearly all live for a time when they will have their homeland, and many have spent their lives trying to recapture that land by force. Most of the Arab states bitterly opposed the founding of Israel and vowed to destroy it. Fighting between Israel and Palestinian guerrillas, and between Israel and its neighbor states, has been a fact of life in the Middle East since Israel was founded.

All of the Middle Eastern countries that have attacked the young state of Israel are themselves young states that have enjoyed real independence only in this century. Until World War I, Turkey held most of the western part of the Arabian peninsula and the lands that bordered the eastern Mediterranean Sea; and

Great Britain held power over eastern Arabia and the Persian Gulf. Most of the modern states of the Middle East did not come into existence until after World War I. Even the ancient country of Egypt was part of the British Empire from 1882 to 1922. When many of these states became independent, the various tribes and religious sects within the newly-defined borders had no history of acting together or of being controlled by any central government. These states have been plagued by internal problems. Even those that have not suffered as much from internal factionalism have had a difficult time, for it takes time for a new nation to develop and mature, and there are always troubles in the process. Although their culture is old, in terms of economics and politics at home and abroad, all the countries of the Middle East are barely adolescent.

Some of these young states have been lucky enough to have a great deal of money to finance their development. Rich oil reserves were discovered in many parts of the Middle East beginning in the 1930's. Since modern technology depends greatly on oil, and since even those developed countries with oil reserves of their own would rather buy oil elsewhere than deplete their own resources, the oil-rich countries of the Middle East have a very marketable commodity. But the presence of vast oil reserves has been another cause of jealousies among the various nations, for some of the countries of the Middle East do not have them. Egypt, for example, has little oil, and Egypt's jealousy of Saudi Arabia's oil riches has affected relations between the two countries. In the 1960's, under President Gamal Abdel Nasser, Egypt backed one faction in a civil war in the Yemen Arab Republic while the Saudis backed the opposing faction.

Another source of tension between the Islamic countries of the Middle East has been their efforts to modernize their industries, improve their communication and transportation networks, and build their trade with other nations. In so doing, they have had a great amount of contact with non-Islamic countries, and this contact has led to changes in their traditional cultures.

For example, Islamic tradition dictates that women must cover their faces with veils. In modernizing countries, however, women were needed in the work force, and women thus received more education. As they became more educated and enjoyed earning money outside the home, they began to question the age-old rules about the role of women, and many took off their veils. The revolution in Iran in 1979 occurred in part because one group of Moslems opposed these changes in their traditions.

The Middle East, because of its rich oil resources and its geographical position at the crossroad between Africa and Asia, plays an important role in world trade and politics. The Suez Canal, built in Egypt in the 1860's by European investors and Egyptian workers, connects the Mediterranean Sea with the Red Sea and remains today an important route for commerce between Europe and the Far East. For economic and political reasons, both the United States and the Soviet Union would like very much to have the countries of the Middle East as allies. Of them all, only Israel is firmly allied with the United States, only Syria is firmly allied with the Soviet Union. Some Arab countries, like Jordan, lean toward the United States in their alliances, while others, like Libya, lean toward the Soviet Union.

Most of the Middle Eastern countries prefer to remain part of the Third World, which is another area not defined by geography. The Third World is composed of nations that are aligned with neither the Western democracies nor the Eastern communist countries and that prefer to remain independent. This nonalignment does not stop the Arab nations of the Middle East from accepting aid from both sides and playing one side against the other.

Most of the Arab countries would like to form a united front in international relations, and over the years there have been several attempts to form organizations and unions for that purpose. Back in 1945, Egypt, Syria, Transjordan (later Jordan), Lebanon, Iraq, and Saudi Arabia formed the Arab League. Its purpose was cooperation in trade and politics. Later, Algeria, Bahrain, Kuwait, Libya, Morocco, Oman, Qatar, the Sudan, Tunisia, the United Arab Emirates, and the Yemen Arab Republic also joined. Wars between Iran and Iraq and between Syria and Jordan, as well as other disputes, have rendered the Arab League largely ineffective, however.

In 1958 Egypt and Syria merged as the United Arab Republic. Its capital was Cairo and its president was Gamal Abdel Nasser. Yemen joined the union that same year and the name was changed to the United Arab States. In 1961, however, a military coup in Syria toppled the leaders who had agreed to merge with Egypt, and Syria withdrew. Yemen soon followed, and that was the end of the union.

In 1964 the Palestine Liberation Organization was formed by the members of the Arab League. Previously, a representative of the Palestinian Arabs had always attended Arab League meetings, but because he represented no recognized government, he did not enjoy full status. The PLO was founded as a coordinating council for the various organizations of Palestinian refugees. It was committed to the dissolution of Israel, mainly through the use of force. Under Yasir Arafat, who gained control of the PLO in 1969, the PLO became a major force in Middle Eastern politics; but by 1983 it was so beset by factionalism that it had lost much of its power.

The most successful Arab organization to date has been the Organization of Petroleum Exporting Countries. Founded in 1973, OPEC also includes several other countries that sell oil. Primarily an economic organization, OPEC meets periodically to set oil prices and production limits. It is also a political group that has occasionally voted to stop sending oil to nations that are allies of Israel. In recent years, political differences and strife among nations that are members of OPEC have weakened the organization, and its members do not always act in concert.

Some kind of pan-Islamic organization that would unite all Islamic nations both spiritually and politically has been a goal since the nineteenth century and has been pursued with particular vigor by Syria and Egypt. The Islamic conference functions somewhat, but thus far the various countries have not been able to resolve their differences and join in a really strong union.

There are so many conflicting forces at work in the Middle East. There are the conflicts between Israel and the Arab nations, between the different Islamic sects within nations like Iran, between the oil-rich and the oil-poor countries, between the philosophies of communism and capitalism, between traditional customs and modern technological progress. Often these struggles have given outside countries (like the United States and the Soviet Union) reasons to intervene, so that they might protect what they see as their own interests. The result has often been that internal problems, which might have been solved had the country been left alone, have escalated into global problems. This is why many people believe that if a third world war occurs, it will begin in the Middle East.

What has happened in the Middle East, what is happening now, and what will happen in the next few years depends in large measure on the men whose biographies are presented in the following chapters. I have chosen these nine men because their decisions have influenced most strongly the current situation in the Middle East and thus have influenced the chances for peace, both in their own region and, to some extent, in the rest of the world.

2

Middle East

Chronology

2

$\diamond$

Seventh century A.D.	The Prophet Mohammed unites the Arab tribes under Islam.
1860's	The Suez Canal is built in Egypt by European investors and Egyptian workers.
1900's (early)	Oil is discovered in Iran.
1917	The British Balfour Declaration supports establishing a Jewish homeland in Palestine.
1922	After World War I, Great Britain is given control over Palestine by the League of Nations.
	Egypt becomes an independent state.
1930's	Major oil-drilling operations begin in the Middle East.
1932	The Kingdom of Saudi Arabia is formed.
1941	Riza Shah Pahlevi, Shah of Iran, is forced out by the British and Russians; his son, Mohammed Riza Pahlevi, becomes Shah.

1944   Syria becomes an independent state.

1945   The Arab League is formed.

1946   Transjordan (now Jordan) is recognized as an independent state.

                       Syria becomes independent.

1947   India is divided and Pakistan is established as a separate nation.

                       The United Nations votes to partition Palestine into an Arab and a Jewish state.

1948   Israel is declared a state; David Ben-Gurion becomes its first prime minister.

                       The combined armies of Egypt, Iraq, Jordan, Lebanon, and Syria invade Israel but are defeated by the Israeli army.

1949   Israel and Jordan agree to a tentative peace.

1951   King Abdullah I of Jordan is assassinated.

                       Libya becomes independent.

1952   King Abdullah's grandson, Prince Hussein, is crowned king of Jordan on his eighteenth birthday.

                       Egypt's King Farouk is deposed.

1953   King ibn Saud of Saudi Arabia dies; Prince Saud becomes king.

1956   Gamal Abdel Nasser becomes president of Egypt; Nasser closes the Suez Canal; British,

French, and Israeli forces invade Egypt; the invading forces withdraw and Egypt reopens the canal.

1958   Egypt and Syria unite as the United Arab Republic; Yemen joins the union, whose name is changed to the United Arab States.

1961   Syria withdraws from the United Arab States, followed by Yemen, and the union is dissolved.

1963   The Baath party establishes control in Syria.

1964   The Palestine Liberation Organization (PLO) is formed by the countries of the Arab League under Nasser.

King Saud of Saudi Arabia dies; Prince Faisal succeeds him.

1967   In the "Six-Day War," Israeli bombers attack airfields in Jordan and Egypt and capture Syria's Golan Heights, Jordan's West Bank, Arab Jerusalem, and the entire Sinai Peninsula; Nasser closes the Suez Canal.

UN resolution 242 calls for Israel to withdraw from all occupied lands, but recognizes the independence of all states, including Israel. Israel refuses to withdraw, and the Arab states refuse to recognize Israel. The PLO gains many converts.

1969   Muammar el-Qaddafi stages a coup and takes over as leader of Libya.

Yasir Arafat becomes chairman of the Palestine Liberation Organization.

1970   After a coup, Hafez el-Assad assumes power in Syria.

English and American bases in Libya are closed; the property of Italians and Jews is confiscated.

Anwar el-Sadat becomes president of Egypt on Nasser's death.

1971   Syria, Egypt, and Libya establish the Federation of Arab Republics.

The PLO is expelled from Jordan and resettles in Lebanon.

1972   Palestinian terrorists massacre eleven Israeli athletes at the Olympic Games in Munich, West Germany.

King Hussein of Jordan suggests a plan for a West Bank-Jordanian federation and is called a Western stooge by his Arab neighbors.

1973   The Organization of Petroleum Exporting Countries (OPEC) is formed.

In the October War, Egypt attacks Israel on Yom Kippur; aided by the United States, Israel repels the invasion.

OPEC declares an oil embargo against the United States.

Libya nationalizes fifty-three percent of the assets of American oil companies.

1974   Arab leaders recognize the Arafat-controlled
                PLO as the legitimate and only representative
                of the Palestinians.

                King Faisal of Saudi Arabia convenes a pan-
                Islamic conference in Cairo.

                East Pakistan gains its independence and is
                renamed Bangladesh.

1975   Anwar el-Sadat of Egypt reopens the Suez
                Canal.

                King Faisal of Saudi Arabia is assassinated;
                Prince Khalid succeeds him.

1976   Syria sends troops into Lebanon to gain
                power there and to attempt to gain control
                of the PLO.

1977   Menachem Begin becomes prime minister of
                Israel.

                Anwar el-Sadat of Egypt is the first Islamic
                leader to visit Israeli-controlled Jerusalem.

1978   Mohammad Zia ul-Haq becomes president of
                Pakistan.

1979   Zulfikar Ali Bhutto, former prime minister
                of Pakistan, is executed.

                The Shah of Iran flees political and religious
                unrest in his country; Ayatollah Ruhollah
                Khomeini returns to Iran after a fourteen-year
                exile; an Islamic Republic is declared; militant

students take over the U.S. embassy in Teheran, Iran, in November, and capture ninety hostages, including sixty-two Americans.

Anwar el-Sadat and Menachem Begin travel to Washington, D.C., in March to sign a peace treaty between Egypt and Israel; eighteen Arab countries impose economic and political sanctions against Egypt.

Mecca's Grand Mosque is seized by armed militant Moslems influenced by the Ayatollah Ruhollah Khomeini; Saudi Arabian forces retake the mosque.

The U.S. Embassy in Islamabad, Pakistan, is burned by Moslems who mistakenly blame the United States for the Grand Mosque takeover.

1980   Iraq invades Iran.

1981   The American hostages in Iran are freed after 444 days in captivity.

Israel bombs PLO installations in Lebanon.

Prince Fahd of Saudi Arabia proposes a Middle East peace plan that implies recognition of Israel; disagreement over the plan leads to the collapse of the November Arab summit meeting in Fez, Morocco.

Anwar el-Sadat is assassinated in October by Moslem militants; Mohamed Hosni Mubarak becomes president.

Israeli forces annex the Golan Heights.

1982   Saudi Arabia and Libya resume diplomatic relations after a fourteen-month break.

            The Egyptian-Libyan border, closed since the signing of the Camp David accords between Sadat and Begin, is reopened.

            King Khalid of Saudi Arabia dies; Prince Fahd succeeds him.

            Israeli forces invade Lebanon in an attempt to rout PLO guerrillas.

            Muammar el-Qaddafi is denied the chairmanship of the Organization of African Unity.

            Lebanese Christian militia, during Israeli occupation of the area, slaughter hundreds of Palestinian refugees in the Beirut refugee camps of Sabra and Shatila.

            President Reagan offers a Middle East peace plan that would allow King Hussein of Jordan to negotiate with Israel on behalf of the Palestinians.

1983   Mutiny in the PLO ranks in May; Yasir Arafat's leadership is threatened.

            Muammar el-Qaddafi is again denied the chairmanship of the Organization of African Unity.

            Libya invades Chad for the third time.

            Menachem Begin announces his resignation; Foreign Minister Yitzhak Shamir succeeds him.

Militant Moslem suicide truck bombs destroy U.S. Marine and French installations in Lebanon.

In December, Yasir Arafat, under siege in Tripoli, Lebanon, by Syrian-backed PLO forces, leaves the country.

3

YASIR

ARAFAT

PLO

Yasir Arafat

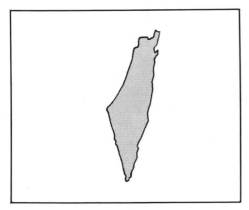

Palestine

3

The problem of what to do with the Palestinian Arab refugees has been a major barrier to peace in the Middle East for more than thirty years; it has thus far defied solution. Yasir Arafat has been the chief spokesman for the Palestinian Arabs for fifteen of those years, and his story is inextricably bound up with the story of the Palestinian struggle for a homeland. Since 1982, Arafat has been engaged in a battle not only for control of the Palestine Liberation Organization but for his very life. If he should lose, the Palestinians may also lose all hope of ever securing the homeland for which they have fought so long.

The ancient land of Palestine on the eastern shore of the Mediterranean Sea is regarded as the Holy Land by Jews, Christians, and Moslems. The Palestinian Arabs trace their origin to the people who lived in the area before the birth of Judaism. These people, the Canaanites—who lived in the lowlands of Canaan, west of the Jordan—are called the pre-Israelites by historians.

Because of its location on the Mediterranean, Palestine was usually the province of some empire. In 70 A.D. it became part of the Roman empire. By 640 it was ruled by Moslems. The European Christian crusaders captured it in 1099. Two hundred years later, Moslem Mamalukes were in power. The Ottoman

Turks conquered Palestine in 1516. They ruled there until World War I, when the British gained control. Palestine was still under British control when Yasir Arafat was born in Egypt, on August 26, 1929.

Arafat's mother, Hamida Khalifa al-Husayni, traced her ancestry through her father back to Fatima, the daughter of the Prophet Mohammed, and thus to the Prophet himself. His father, Abdul Rauf al-Qudwa, came from a family of wealthy merchants and traders whose ancestors had settled in the late 1700's in the area of Palestine called Gaza. Abdul Rauf and Hamida were married in Jerusalem in 1917.

Arafat's father was a merchant, like others in his family. In Gaza his customers included Jews, who had begun to emigrate to Palestine from Europe in the late 1800's. These Jews claimed Palestine as their home. It was there that Judaism was born and that a Hebrew kingdom flourished until 70 A.D., when the Romans destroyed the sacred temple in Jerusalem and drove the Hebrews out. Although he spoke with hate about the Jews in private, he did not let his personal feelings interfere with his business, and he profited through his trade with the Jews.

By the time World War I broke out, Jews from Europe were calling for the establishment of a homeland in Palestine. The British were sympathetic to the Jewish cause, and in 1917, the year Abdul Rauf and Hamida were married, the British Balfour Declaration supported the establishment of a Jewish home in Palestine, provided it would not "prejudice the civil and religious rights" of the non-Jewish Palestinians. The Palestinian Arabs bitterly opposed this plan, and there were frequent clashes between Jews and Arabs in the region. Many Arabs resented the merchants who traded with Jews, and eventually Abdul Rauf was forced to flee from Gaza with his family.

Yasir Arafat was born in Cairo, where his father continued the family business. Their fifth child, he was born Rahman Abdul Rauf Arafat al-Qudwa al-Husayni, but we will call him Yasir.

Young Yasir was quiet and withdrawn, noticeably different from the other children. Whenever possible, he would avoid a fight, but if he got caught in an unavoidable tussle he would not fight back or cry out in his own defense. Instead, he would stare down his attackers. He had inherited large, protruding eyes from his mother, and his steady, penetrating gaze was so intense that his assailants would soon back off.

During his years growing up in Cairo, Yasir spent most of his time in religious training. Although all Arab boys are schooled in the Islamic religion, Yasir spent extra time studying the Koran. He and his brothers received their religious instruction from their mother's uncle, Yusuf Awad al-Akbar, who noticed Yasir's special interest and encouraged it. Akbar was very proud of his family's connection to the Prophet Mohammed; he felt superior to Yasir's father and taught Yasir that his mother's blessed bloodline made him and all of her other children superior to their father. By Arab tradition, fathers have little to do with the upbringing of their sons until they reach adolescence, so Yasir had little opportunity to know his father. He seemed distant and cold, and Yasir felt little loyalty toward him. He bestowed his loyalty on Yusuf Awad al-Akbar instead and found it easy to believe his great-uncle's criticisms of his father. No doubt Abdul Rauf was aware of Akbar's feelings and resented the older man's influence with his sons, but at that time—in the late 1930's—he did nothing about it.

Abdul Rauf was more concerned about the situation in Palestine than with family jealousies. Jewish influence in Palestine was growing. Money from Europe and America was helping to finance the developing Zionist movement, a worldwide movement whose goal was the establishment of a Jewish state in Palestine. Skilled Jews were moving to Palestine with the intention of making it their permanent home, and the Jewish communities there flourished. The resentment of the Palestinians grew as they saw not only the steady stream of Jewish immigrants flowing into the country but also the better standard of living that the Jewish communities seemed to enjoy. Abdul Rauf al-Qudwa traveled often on business between Cairo, Gaza, and Jerusalem, and he came home with stories about violence between Jews and Arabs in Palestine and charges that the Jews were robbing the Arab Palestinians of their land.

Although he did not feel close to his father, young Yasir paid attention to the older man's angry speeches against the Jews. He knew that his father was becoming involved in the growing Palestinian resistance to a Jewish takeover and that he had joined

a faction of the militant Moslem organization, the Moslem Brotherhood, that was determined to keep Palestine for the Arab
Palestinians. Apparently Yasir's father used his connection
with the Brotherhood to settle a personal account. In 1939, after
a family quarrel, Yusuf al-Akbar was found murdered, his body
marked with the Brotherhood symbol.

The Egyptian police questioned Abdul Rauf about the death
of his wife's uncle, and the leaders of the Moslem Brotherhood
decided that as long as he remained in Cairo, he would be constantly watched by the police. He would be more useful to them
elsewhere. Accordingly, in 1939, not long after the murder,
Abdul Rauf moved his family from Cairo back to Gaza. There he
began to organize a cell, or unit, of the Moslem Brotherhood.
He recruited a young schoolteacher from southern Lebanon,
Majid Halaby, to organize the Palestinian boys of Gaza into a
sort of junior guerrilla unit, and in order to demonstrate his own
commitment to Palestinian resistance, he pledged his own sons
as the group's first members. Yasir Arafat had been despondent
since the death of his great-uncle, and his father no doubt believed that membership in the young guerrilla movement would
take his son's mind off the tragedy.

It was Majid Halaby who started to call Yasir Arafat by the
nickname of "Yasir," after Yasir al-Birah, a Palestinian who had
died in the struggle against the Jews and British in Palestine.
Halaby had been a protégé of Yasir al-Birah, and the young
Arafat reminded him of his former mentor in both looks and
manner. After a while, everyone except his father was calling him
"Yasir," and young Yasir Arafat had transferred the devotion he
had felt for his great-uncle to his new teacher.

Halaby called the Palestinian Arabs who fought against the
Jews and the British "Fedayeen," an Arabic word that means
"men of sacrifice." He taught his young charges that the cause of
the Palestinians was more important than their own individual
lives, and Yasir accepted that idea without question. Eventually he
moved out of his father's house and went to live with Halaby.
He became Halaby's chief assistant, and when Halaby decided
to take a group of the boys to Jerusalem so they could gain firsthand experience in guerrilla fighting, Yasir was among them.
The older men in the Brotherhood felt that the boys were too

young and inexperienced and tried to prevent the excursion. When Halaby defied them, they arranged to have him killed. They told the boys that he had been killed in the line of duty, but Yasir suspected otherwise.

Yasir took Halaby's death very hard; he brooded over it for months. Although it was much later that his suspicions about the circumstances of Halaby's death were confirmed, Yasir at once decided to devote his life to continuing Halaby's work. Unfortunately, he was not quite sure how to go about it. Varying views on politics and religion had splintered the Palestinian Arabs into many factions, and in this confused atmosphere, Yasir was unable to distinguish any particular political or moral philosophy. All he knew was that Palestine needed to be protected from the Jews and the British.

Yasir's militant feelings grew in intensity as the Jews became more determined to have a state of their own. The terrible reign of Adolf Hitler in Europe and the atrocities committed against Jews during World War II had caused many more Jews to migrate to Palestine. Faced with Arab resistance groups like the Moslem Brotherhood, the Jews in Palestine organized the Irgun, an extremist group whose purpose was to win a Palestine homeland for the Jews, by force if necessary. The atrocities of the war had also swayed world opinion in favor of the Jewish cause, and it was clear that the United Nations would vote to partition Palestine and thus give the Jews their state of Israel. In cities like Jerusalem there was open fighting between Jews and Arabs. Determined to do as much as he could to stop the Jews, Yasir went to Jerusalem to offer his services to the Palestinian guerrillas there.

Just as eighteen-year-old Yasir Arafat arrived in Jerusalem, the United Nations voted to partition Palestine. The plan that was adopted by the General Assembly on November 29, 1947, called for Palestine to be divided into two states—one Jewish and the other Arab—and a small internationally administered zone that was to include the city of Jerusalem. Under this plan, 26,000 square miles, fifty-six percent of the land, was to be given to the Jewish state of Israel.

The stunned Palestinians refused to acknowledge the right of the UN to make such a profound decision. They felt that the creation of Israel from Palestine was an illegal and arrogant act by foreign oppressors. The various Palestinian guerrilla organizations could not agree on a way to fight the UN resolution; they were in too much disarray. All over Palestine people who faced displacement reacted with fear and anger. Palestinians living on the lands that had been given to Israel refused to move to the lands that had been designated for them; on the other hand, they could not remain where they were. Soon a huge human flood of refugees crossed the borders into Jordan and Syria.

The rest of the Arab world was as much against the UN resolution as the Palestinians were, and they agreed with the Palestinians that there could be no compromise on the matter. In 1948 forces from Egypt, Jordan, Syria, Lebanon, and Iraq marched into Palestine and attacked the Jews, intent upon reclaiming the land for the Palestinians. Yasir Arafat joined the invading Egyptian army for a time. He carried supplies and water and helped out in noncombat areas. Victory eluded the Arabs, however, as the Israeli army beat back the invading armies and pushed them back across the borders to their own countries. By January 1949 when a truce was finally declared, Israel had lost none of its own territory and had increased its holdings by about one half, including west Jerusalem, which was supposed to have been a neutral zone. Yasir Arafat was dismayed. He had believed that the power of the Arab armies would bring justice to the Palestinians. Instead he saw defeat. Brokenhearted, he returned to his family home in Gaza. But by July of 1948 the fighting between Arabs and Jews in Gaza was so widespread that Yasir's father once again feared for the safety of his family and moved them back to their house in Cairo.

Yasir was nineteen by now. He enrolled in a technological high school and became fascinated with the manufacture of explosives. The school's teachers were either members of or sympathizers of the Moslem Brotherhood and they used the school's facilities and the abilities of their students to make homemade bombs. Yasir learned quickly and was happy to make explosives for use against Israel. He paid little attention to his academic studies. Meanwhile, his father had rejoined the Moslem Brotherhood, and in January 1949, he was asked to return to Gaza to continue organizing Palestinians against Israel. The family went back to Gaza, and Yasir worked with his brothers to recruit young Palestinians to the cause.

Since the Arab groups had refused the land given them under the UN resolution, taking an all-or-nothing stance, King Abdullah of Transjordan—as Jordan was called then—took advantage of the situation and took over the central hill region of Palestine, called the West Bank. Now the Palestinians had two enemies: the Jews and the Jordanians. The Palestinians were in no position to declare war on Jordan; but they did attack the Jordanians on the West Bank. They also sent some of the young members of their movement to Egypt for guerrilla training. Yasir was among them. He returned to Gaza in the summer of 1949.

Arafat immediately put to use what he had learned in Egypt. In Gaza, some Palestinians, who were homeless and dispossessed, favored the annexation of the West Bank by Jordan because they wanted to become Jordanian citizens. Arafat, who believed that the West Bank belonged to the Palestinians, led a young band of guerrillas throughout Gaza attacking, terrorizing, and murdering Palestinians who favored the Jordanian move. His efforts made little difference, however, and the annexation of the West Bank by Jordan was completed in 1950.

Shortly afterward, in the summer of 1950, Arafat yielded to his father's persuasion and returned to Cairo to pursue a university education. He enrolled in the civil engineering course at the University of Cairo, but again devoted little time to his academic studies. He became an important organizer for the Moslem Brotherhood on campus and, in 1952, founded the Palestinian Student Federation, whose purpose was to work against Israel and for the restoration of Palestine to the Palestinians. At the same time, the people of Egypt were growing restless under the government of King Farouk and his mother, Queen Nazli, and Arafat decided to contribute to the unrest by staging marches and protests against various branches of the government. The police responded with violent tactics, and in protest against the police brutality, the people of Cairo took to the streets in large numbers, burning and looting. It was against this background of civil unrest in 1952 that Gamal Abdel Nasser and a group of army officers overthrew the Egyptian monarchy.

Internal problems and political differences within the Palestinian Student Federation came to a head in the fall of 1953 when the Arafat-led faction was voted out of the group. Arafat immediately formed a rival organization, the Palestine Student Union. One of the members of the new PSU had access to a printing plant, and Yasir Arafat learned to write public declarations of his organization's beliefs and intentions. Distributed as leaflets, these manifestos spread the word about Arafat and his revolutionary plans, and membership in the PSU grew dramatically. In 1955, after receiving more training from the Egyptian Army in the tactics of guerrilla warfare, Arafat took steps to unify the various Palestinian student organizations. When the Palestinian Student Federation resisted his efforts, some of the officers of that group were killed; after that the PSF agreed to cooperate with Arafat. He created the General Union of Palestinian Students (GUPS) and was elected chairman. He was then twenty-six years old.

Once Gamal Abdel Nasser was in power, Arafat and other Palestinians counted on his support in the struggle for Palestine. Nasser backed guerrilla raids on Israel and trained Palestinian fighters. He took an independent stance with the European countries and the United States. In 1956, after Great Britain and the U.S. refused to give Egypt help in financing the Aswan Dam, Nasser nationalized the Suez Canal. But Israel, which had been denied use of the canal since 1950, took advantage of the ill will between Nasser and the West and invaded Egypt. Although Egypt continued to deny Israel the use of the canal, what remained in Arafat's mind was the idea that the Egyptians had again been humiliated by Israeli forces. In disgust he declared that the Palestinians must stand on their own and not depend on the improperly prepared forces of other Arab states. Members of the Moslem Brotherhood reacted even more strongly to the defeat, and when they learned that Nasser planned to outlaw their organization, they began to plot his assassination.

In March 1957 Communist-bloc countries invited several Arab countries to send delegates to an international student convention in Prague, the capital of Czechoslovakia. Arafat led an eight-member delegation representing the General Union of

Palestinian Students. While in Prague, the delegation split into two factions, and five of the students returned to Cairo, leaving Arafat and two fellow students, named Khalil al-Wazir and Salah Khalef, behind.

When the five students arrived back in Cairo, they were immediately arrested and questioned by the Egyptian secret police, who had discovered the plot to assassinate Nasser and believed that the GUPS might have knowledge of the plot. The police told the students that they had evidence tying Arafat to the planned assassination attempt, and as soon as the students were released they sent him word that if he returned to Cairo, he faced certain arrest.

Arafat, Wazir, and Khalef decided not to return to Cairo. Wazir had several cousins enrolled at the University of Stuttgart in West Germany, where there was a large Palestinian student population. He contacted his relatives, and with their help, the three managed to reach West Germany. They traveled with borrowed passports, pasting their photographs over those of Palestinian students who were actually enrolled at Stuttgart. For Arafat, Stuttgart was just a brief stopover; he wanted to be in the Middle East.

One day he noticed an ad in a German newspaper for workers to go to Kuwait, a tiny, oil-rich nation on the Persian Gulf, that was in the midst of a building boom and needed skilled laborers. The ad made it clear that the Kuwaiti government was especially interested in hiring Arab workers. Arafat applied for and got one of the jobs.

While working for the Department of Water Supply in Kuwait, the industrious Arafat started his own construction company and hired other Palestinians to work for him. He has said that if he hadn't been a revolutionary he could have become a billionaire in Kuwait, as did many Palestinians. However, he had dedicated his life to winning back Palestine, and he was soon organizing a movement in Kuwait. By the fall of 1959, he had raised enough money to publish a newspaper, a small handbill called *Our Palestine*. Six months later, Arafat went to Lebanon to tour the Palestinian refugee camps there and to set up a distribution system for his newspaper. He was shocked by conditions in the camps. For the first time he came face to face with the cold reality of life in them, with the squalor and degradation of the unfortunate inhabitants. He returned to Kuwait more determined than ever to dedicate his life to the liberation of Palestine. He worked day and night to make his organization, el-Fatah, strong enough to accomplish that goal.

In May 1964 the countries of the Arab League, under the leadership of Gamal Abdel Nasser, formed the Palestine Libera- tion Organization (PLO). The act infuriated Arafat. He de- manded to know what right Nasser had to form a "Palestinian" organization. Nasser, who had not forgotten that Arafat had been implicated in the Moslem Brotherhood plot to assassinate him, ordered his secret police to kill Arafat, who was forced to go underground for several months. He continued to publish *Our Palestine* from his hiding places and surfaced at last in Jordan, under the protection and sponsorship of King Hussein, who, like other Arab leaders, was trying very hard to present a united Arab front to the rest of the world, especially Israel.

Operating from bases in Jordan, and with the financial and military support of the Jordanian government, el-Fatah launched numerous guerrilla raids against Israeli border settlements. At the same time, border incidents increased between Israel and Syria and Israel and Egypt. In June 1967, Israel launched a full- scale war against Jordan, Syria, and Egypt, capturing Egypt's Sinai Peninsula, part of Syria's Golan Heights, and the Old City of Jerusalem, which Jordan had annexed in the late 1940's. Various Palestinian guerrilla groups, including Arafat's el-Fatah, also suffered serious setbacks during this Six-Day War, which was so decisive that Arafat despaired of ever making progress in his campaign against Israel.

Then, in March 1968, an incident occurred that altered once again the situation in the Middle East. A busload of Israeli children were injured when a mine that had been placed by guerrillas exploded. Israel retaliated by invading Jordan and attacking the Palestinian guerrilla camps there. The Jordanian army resisted the Israelis and a pitched battle resulted in much bloodshed on both sides. The Israelis failed to dismantle the guerrilla camps in Jordan, and their invasion of Jordan had the effect of focusing world attention on el-Fatah and Yasir Arafat. Arafat took advantage of the attention to increase the influence of el-Fatah in the PLO. He was successful, and by February 1969 he had managed to gain control of the PLO and was named its chairman.

The PLO, a confederation of Palestinian resistance groups, grew dramatically under his leadership, and Arafat soon felt powerful enough to speak out against King Hussein, whom he considered too moderate. He began publicly demanding more radical actions from the Jordanians, and Hussein responded by deciding that the PLO presence in Jordan had become intolerable. In the fall of 1970 Hussein declared war on the Fedayeen, the "men of sacrifice." Many thousands were killed, and in 1971 the PLO was driven out of Jordan into Syria and Lebanon. Arafat set up new headquarters in Lebanon and concentrated on establishing ties with guerrilla and revolutionary movements the world over. With support from China and the Soviet Union, he continued his guerrilla activities against Israel from bases in southern Lebanon.

One of Arafat's purposes was to harass Israel enough to provoke another war between the Israelis and the Arab states, but his activities had little to do with the October War of 1973. Anwar el-Sadat, Gamal Abdel Nasser's successor, was the chief architect of this campaign against Israel.

On October 6, 1973, which was Yom Kippur, the holiest day in the Jewish year, a combined Arab force launched a two-pronged assault on Israel. Egyptian forces struck eastward across the Suez Canal while Syrian forces advanced from the north. Although the Israelis were caught unawares, and although Iraq, Jordan, Libya, and several other Arab states supported Egypt and Syria, the Arab forces were unable to gain any territory. The war, however, restored Arab pride in their military forces and consolidated Arab support behind Sadat.

Sadat called for a united Arab effort on behalf of the Palestinians, and the leaders of the Arab world passed a resolution calling the PLO the legitimate and only representative of the Palestinians. As the chief spokesman for the Palestinian cause, Arafat was invited to address the General Assembly of the United Nations in November 1974.

When he stepped to the podium to deliver his speech, Arafat received a standing ovation. Dressed in a khaki jacket, wearing a checkered *kaffiyeh*—the Arab headdress—and with a holstered gun on his hip, Arafat hailed the Fedayeen cause and the determination of the Palestinian people to win back their ancestral land. His speech was greeted with thunderous applause. The United Nations that welcomed Yasir Arafat was a vastly different organization from the one that had partitioned Palestine twenty-seven years before. Many of the nations assembled there in 1974 had won their independence through revolution and were sympathetic to Arafat and the Palestinians.

Until 1982, Yasir Arafat retained his position as the unquestioned leader of the PLO and the chief spokesman for the Palestinian people. El-Fatah, the organization he had founded in Kuwait, remained the largest and strongest of the eight groups in the PLO, claiming the allegiance of eighty percent of PLO members. Between 1974 and 1980, from bases in Syria and Lebanon, Palestinian guerrillas carried out scores of deadly raids against Israeli border settlements, crossing the borders under cover of darkness to plant mines, ambush patrols, throw grenades, and place bombs. But they failed to win back any territory.

Meanwhile, all efforts by concerned parties to establish a Palestinian homeland through negotiation were unavailing. Arafat refused to recognize Israel as a legitimate state, and the Israelis refused to recognize the PLO as the legitimate representative of the Palestinian people. Under these circumstances, there was no possibility of peace negotiations between the two.

As the years wore on, the entire Middle East region suffered from the unrest, and many Arab leaders were eager for some sort of negotiated solution. Syria's president, Hafez el-Assad, chose to try to gain influence through force. In 1976 he sent troops into Lebanon to try to gain power over the PLO and thus make both sides deal with him if they wanted a comprehensive peace settlement. Although Arafat personally distrusted Assad, he wanted to keep Syria's support, and so publicly he treated the Syrian president as an ally.

Other Arab leaders sought a more moderate route than Assad's. In 1981 Prince Fahd of Saudi Arabia proposed a plan that upheld the Arab demands for a Palestinian state but implied Arab recognition of Israel's right to exist. Arafat surprised nearly everyone by describing the plan as "a good beginning." Some observers took the comment to be an indication that Arafat, too, was growing tired of the impasse in the Middle East and was more inclined to pursue the route of negotiation. Israel and Syria opposed the Fahd plan, however, as did the more radical elements of el-Fatah, and the Fahd plan never got off the ground.

In the meantime, Israel had decided to take action to end the PLO's constant sniping against her border settlements. On June 16, 1982, the Israelis launched an all-out attack on PLO positions in Lebanon. The awesome invasion destroyed the main guerrilla bases, and thousands of Palestinians were killed. Although the PLO resisted the Israeli forces for several weeks, Arafat was eventually forced to agree to withdraw his forces from Lebanon. In August, under the watchful eyes of a multinational security force, some 3500 PLO troops were dispersed to Tunisia, the Sudan, and southern Yemen. Arafat himself set sail for Greece, where the newly elected leftist government assured him security and protection. Since Syria still controlled areas of southern and eastern Lebanon and continued to be one of the major suppliers of money and military equipment to the PLO, it might have seemed the logical place for him to go. Arafat wanted to maintain his independence from Syria, however, and particularly from its president, Hafez el-Assad.

Meanwhile, the Israelis continued their campaign to drive all PLO guerrillas from Lebanon. They were assisted in the occupation of PLO refugee camps in Lebanon by Lebanese Christian militias, and in September some of those troops slaughtered hundreds of Palestinian refugees in the camps of Sabra and Shatila. The massacre was denounced all over the world, even people in Israel protested their government's policies. The PLO and Yasir Arafat benefited; world opinion seemed to regard them as valiant underdogs.

There was sympathy for the PLO in the United States, and in the fall of 1982 President Ronald Reagan put forth a Middle East peace initiative aimed at solving the Palestinian problem. The plan called for a Jordanian-Palestinian association (the name Palestine being used to mean the Israeli-occupied West Bank and Gaza Strip). Jordan's King Hussein would represent the Palestinians in peace talks with Israel (since Israel refused to negotiate with the PLO or to recognize it as a legitimate organization). Since Yasir Arafat had devoted much of his life to the cause of an independent Palestine, it came as a surprise to many observers when he said he found "some positive elements" in the Reagan plan and agreed to talks with Hussein. Arafat is a complex man, and he is not the first militant Middle East leader to moderate his stance. Egypt's Anwar Sadat hated Israel until his brother was killed in the October War. His brother's death caused him to feel revulsion at the thought of any more bloodshed. The massacre of Palestinian refugees in Sabra and Shatila may have had a similar effect on Yasir Arafat. The discussions of the Reagan Plan soon bogged down, however. Israel completely rejected the plan, and Arafat was having trouble finding support for it from his own PLO.

President Assad of Syria was against the Reagan plan, and he played on the fears of radical PLO elements that Arafat might be persuaded to accept a settlement that denied the Palestinians an independent homeland. Assad sent Palestinian forces into the Syrian- controlled areas of northern and eastern Lebanon, and it was in eastern Lebanon, in mid-May 1983, that radical elements of el-Fatah staged a mutiny against their leader.

At first Arafat downplayed the rebellion, but over the next few weeks it grew into a series of full-scale shootouts between the opposing factions. Arafat, who had stayed away from Lebanon since the previous August, had no choice but to return to try to reestablish control. This meant that since Syria held the PLO strongholds in Lebanon, he would have to modify his position of independence from Syria and Assad.

Arafat put off going to Damascus, but by late June he gave in and at the request of other PLO leaders, traveled to the Syrian capital. The other leaders believed that the only way to reunify the organization was to mend the rift between Arafat and Assad, but within a week both men knew that compromise was impossible. Assad banished Arafat from Damascus, which was a humiliating insult to the chairman of the PLO.

By October 1983 Arafat had lost control of the PLO and was on the run. Syrian-backed PLO factions had launched an assault on the PLO forces that remained loyal to him, and by November Arafat and his loyalists were making a last-ditch stand in the Lebanese port of Tripoli. While rumors abounded that he would somehow escape, Arafat declared that he would stay with his people, no matter what happened. He left Lebanon, along with his troops, in December.

Arafat still had the support of most of the Palestinian refugees, for whom he had been a father figure for fifteen years. The well-to-do businessmen in Kuwait and other Arab countries, not to mention the inhabitants of the refugee camps, recognized that it was he who had transformed the Palestinian cause into an international issue and made the Palestinians a force to be reckoned with. It was he who, if he could have maintained the unity of the PLO, might have been able to negotiate the return of at least some of the Palestinians' land. A confederation with Jordan would have been a far cry from the Palestinian state for which he had fought for so long, but after so many decades of dispersion and struggle, some Palestinians believed that it was better than nothing at all. Arafat had not always pursued a steady course as leader of the PLO: he had entered into alliances with extremist groups and militant Arab nations; he had tolerated corruption and incompetence among his subordinates; but he had been personally incorruptible and totally committed to his people. Those who supported him were not so well armed nor so well organized as the Syrians. As their leader fought for his life, they were powerless to help him.

The future of Yasir Arafat, of the PLO, of the Palestinians, and of the Middle East is up in the air. Negotiations involving the Palestinians have stalled. No plan for peace can proceed without the Palestinians, and until the question of PLO leadership is resolved, there will be no recognized spokesman for them. Yasir Arafat may yet emerge victorious, or he may find it necessary to negotiate with Hafez el-Assad of Syria in order to maintain a position of leadership in the PLO. On the other hand, he may lose everything. If he does, he will be remembered by history as a tragic figure, one who came close to accomplishing his objective, but saw it elude him in the end. An historian at the American University in Beirut summed it up when he remarked to a reporter for *The New York Times*: "Poor man, Arafat. No, more importantly, poor Palestinian people."

4

HAFEZ
EL-ASSAD

Syria

Hafez el-Assad

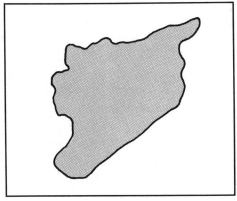

Syria

4

Hafez el-Assad is president of Syria, a country about the size of North Dakota. It borders on Lebanon and the Mediterranean Sea on the west, on Turkey on the north and northwest, on Iraq on the east and south, and on Jordan and Israel on the southwest. Its population of about ten million is predominantly Moslem, but about fifteen percent of its people are Christians. The government of Syria is socialist, and the state controls most of the industry and commerce. Since the 1950's the country has had close ties with the Soviet Union.

Syria occupies a central position in the Middle East—geographically and politically. It shares a border with Israel and has long been a place for Palestinian refugees. Because of its location on the Mediterranean, it is an important trade conduit: Petroleum pipelines from both Jordan and Iraq cross Syria. Until about 1982, however, Syria was not considered a major force in the Middle East. The reason for the change is Hafez el-Assad. He has managed to maneuver himself into a position where he could greatly influence that troubled area. By the fall of 1983, it was clear that any Middle East peace plan would have to take into account Assad's interests; and, in fact, peace of any kind would depend greatly on him. As of that time, Assad controlled strong factions of the Palestinian Liberation Organization, was actively seeking the annexation of Lebanon and was directly involved in that country's war, and was in a position to influence U.S. military policy in the Middle East.

Hafez el-Assad, whose name means "protector of lions," was born in either 1928 or 1930—depending on the source—in the province of Latakia, in what is now northwestern Syria. He was the oldest son in a family that owned its own land and earned its livelihood by farming.

Assad's family belonged to the Alawite sect, a faction of Shiite Moslems that predominated in the area around the seaport city of Latakia. A secretive community, the Alawites blended nature worship and Christianity with Islam. The majority were peasants and farming people with a strong sense of independence. Looked down on by the majority population of Sunni Moslems— especially those who lived in cities—Alawites were proud of their ties to the land and wanted that land to be free of foreign domination.

Throughout most of its history, that land had been under the control of one group of outsiders after another. For many years before World War I, the Ottoman Turks ruled the region; but in 1920, after the Turks were defeated in the war, France was given a League of Nations mandate over the land encompassing the present-day nations of Syria and Lebanon. Back then the entire region was called Syria. In 1926 a tiny section of the area—less than one fifteenth—was made into the separate state of Lebanon. By about 1930, the rest of the area was generally recognized as the state of Syria. Both, however, were still under French control.

Assad's family, like most people in Syria, did not feel that the state of Lebanon should have been created; they felt that the division was artificial and arbitrary. They blamed the French and hoped one day not only to be free of French domination but also to see Lebanon and Syria reunited as Syria. Assad grew up hearing these opinions.

Assad attended elementary school in his native town of Qardaha and then enrolled in the scientific section of the Latakia secondary school. By the time he entered high school, a new political party had arisen. The Baath party, whose formal name translates as "Arab Socialist Renaissance party," called for public ownership of the means of production, land redistribution, and freedom from foreign domination. Central to its philosophy was its hope for the unification of all Arab lands into one nation, ending the hodgepodge of separate states created by the League of Nations. Members of the Alawite sect joined the new party in large numbers, and Hafez el-Assad was among them.

One of Syria's first actions as an independent nation was to join other Arab states in their unsuccessful attack on the new state of Israel in 1948. When Palestinian refugees began pouring out of Israel, Syria accepted many of them, but made them live in refugee camps. Otherwise, the first few years of the new nation of Syria were marked mostly by internal disagreements. In 1949 alone, three different governments were established and then overthrown. It would be many years before Syria enjoyed a stable government.

Hafez el-Assad completed secondary school in 1952 and enrolled at Homs Military Academy. From there, he went to the air academy, graduating in 1955 as a pilot officer with the rank of lieutenant. Three years later, he went to the Soviet Union for further training, not as a member of the Syrian military establishment, but as a member of the united forces of the United Arab Republic (UAR).

Gamal Abdel Nasser was the major force in the formation of the UAR. In 1952 General Nasser led the overthrow of Egypt's King Farouk and in 1956 became that country's second president. Nasser believed that Farouk had been too much influenced by Britain, whose possession Egypt had been from 1882 to 1922. The new government looked to the Soviet Union, rather than to the West, for support. Nasser persuaded Syria that the two countries would be more powerful if they joined, and the United Arab Republic was formed in 1958, with its capital in Cairo. The Soviet Union offered to train the military forces of the UAR, and that same year Lieutenant Assad went to Russia for special training in nighttime air combat. The following year he was assigned to duty in Cairo as a squadron leader in the UAR Air Force. While there, he became the leader of a secret group of Syrian officers called the Military Committee, which supported the Baath party and hoped one day to bring it to power in the UAR.

In September 1961, Syria, feeling itself only a satellite of Egypt, withdrew from the UAR and established the Syrian Arab Republic. Assad opposed the secession and in December was removed from the armed forces and assigned to a civilian post.

While no longer formally in the military, Assad maintained his ties with the secret Military Committee, which, with others in the Baath party, began to work for the overthrow of the secessionist government. A coup took place on March 8, 1963, which gave the Baath party control of the Syrian government. Assad was restored to his military position and appointed commander of the Syrian Air Force; by December 1964 he had also attained the rank of general.

The Baath party, once it seized power, fell prey to factionalism. Men who had worked together to get power were unable to agree about how to use it. A radical element in the party wanted to reestablish strong ties with Egypt and the Soviet Union, while the more moderate party leaders hoped to pursue a more independent course. At first Assad supported the moderates, but he later switched his allegiance to the radicals, who then felt strong enough to stage their own coup. The moderate leadership fell on February 23, 1966, and Assad's reward for supporting the new regime was his appointment as minister of defense; he also kept his position as commander of the air force.

Assad held these positions when Israel attacked Egypt, Jordan, and Syria in the June 1967 Six-Day War. When the war ended, two thirds of the Syrian Air Force lay in shambles on the ground and Israel occupied an area of Syria on the Israeli border, northeast of the Sea of Galilee, called the Golan Heights. Assad held himself responsible for these losses.

From then on, Assad's major goal was to rebuild Syrian forces and to strengthen Syria's ties with its Arab neighbors in order to regain the territories Israel had captured. Others in the Baath party did not have the same priorities. Major General Salah al-Jadid, who had been a member of the Military Committee in Cairo and who had collaborated with Assad in the 1966 coup, wanted to concentrate on changing Syria's economy to conform to the socialist principles the Baath party had long favored. The factions led by Assad and Jadid clashed several times, and in

February 1969 Assad tried to seize control of the government. He backed off, however, when the Soviet Union, which favored Jadid, threatened to cut off all military and economic aid to Syria if he succeeded.

The situation came to a head in 1970. In September, in the neighboring state of Jordan, King Hussein ordered an attack on the Palestine Liberation Organization guerrillas within Jordan's borders. Jadid, who was assistant secretary-general of the Baath Party, ordered Syrian troops to aid those PLO forces. Assad, believing that this was a mistake on Syria's part, refused to provide air support for the Syrian troops. In the power struggle that followed, the army remained loyal to Assad, and he was able to oust Jadid. The coup, accomplished without bloodshed, occurred on November 13, 1970, and Assad ordered Jadid into exile in Egypt.

Hafez el-Assad was the only candidate in the election for president that was held four months later, and in March 1971 he became the first Alawite president of Syria. He immediately set about making changes in his country. He allowed the people and the press more freedom than they had enjoyed before, including more political rights and the freedom to travel outside the country. He encouraged private enterprise, although the state continued to own the large industries and banks. He raised wages and lowered prices on basic food items. His goal was a society that was more socialist than communist, one that was more liberal and flexible than the type of government the Soviet Union championed.

In foreign affairs, he increased trade with other countries and took steps to improve relations with his Arab neighbors, especially Egypt. Assad continued to believe that the Arabs should unite as a single nation. Relations between Syria and Egypt had been strained since the breakup of the UAR. Gamal Abdel Nasser had died in 1970, and Assad forged a new alliance with Nasser's successor, Anwar el-Sadat. The armed forces of the two countries were put under a single command, and in September 1971, Syria, Egypt, and Libya joined in what became the Federation of Arab Republics. In 1972 Assad went to Moscow and secured guarantees of Soviet military and economic aid, but he also made it clear that he did not intend to be a puppet of the Soviet Union.

Although many Syrians supported Assad's actions, there was a deep resentment about the number of Alawites, members of the Baath party, and relatives of Assad in his government. They made up half the Syrian army and occupied most of the top positions in the army and the government. Assad resisted all attempts to change this situation. Perhaps because he had seen so many coups and so much treachery, he had decided that the only safe course was to have people around him with whom he had personal and blood ties. At this writing, his brother, a nephew, a cousin, and a brother-in-law all hold high positions in the Syrian armed forces.

It is important to remember that in Syria Sunni Moslems make up the majority of the population, while Shiite Alawites comprise only twelve percent. Some of the Sunnis worried that Assad and his government might try to weaken the power of Islam in Syria. When, in early 1973, the proposed new constitution, instead of declaring Islam the country's official religion, pledged respect for and freedom of practice for all faiths, Islamic traditionalists rioted. In response to the disturbances, Assad added an article to the proposed constitution that required any Syrian head of state to be a Moslem. The amended constitution was adopted by an overwhelming majority of voters in March of that year. But that didn't satisfy the zealots. The following month there were new riots in Damascus and Aleppo, and that summer Assad ordered about forty army officers (all Sunni Moslems) executed for allegedly plotting to assassinate him.

Assad quieted his enemies for a while when he joined with Egypt in attacking Israel on Yom Kippur 1973, in an attempt to regain the lands Israel had captured in the Six-Day War in 1967. King Hussein of Jordan, with whom Assad had also worked to improve relations, sent an armored unit to help the Syrian forces. While the Israelis, with U.S. help, managed to hold on to the territories they still occupied, the Syrians, like the Egyptians, felt new respect for the abilities of their fighting forces and gained the support of other Arab states. By the terms of the negotiated truce, which Assad finally agreed to sign in late May 1974, Syria recovered part of the Golan Heights. Assad had hoped for a return of all of the territory and was determined to get it back eventually, one way or another.

Diplomatic relations between Syria and the United States, broken off after the 1967 Six-Day War, resumed in June 1974, and western leaders hoped that Assad would rely less on the Soviet Union for military and economic aid. Assad then appeared to be a moderate leader who was concerned about the rights of the Palestinians but did not call for the destruction of Israel, who preferred to work toward his goals by negotiation not by force, and who saw no reason not to work with both the United States and the Soviet Union, as long as Syria benefited. United States reporters described him as a "solid man," who looked more like a schoolteacher than a military man. They described his look as "kindly" and noted that he was married and the father of five children. They called him "an extremely prudent manager who carefully consults his associates before making decisions." Only Henry Kissinger suggested that there might be a more reckless side to Assad than most other Americans had seen. As United States Secretary of State, Kissinger had helped to negotiate the 1974 settlement between Israel and the Arab states that had attacked her. He knew from firsthand experience that Assad could be difficult and that he had compromised on the return of the Golan Heights only with great reluctance. In his memoirs Kissinger said of Assad: "I have known negotiators who put one foot over the edge. He was the only one who would actually jump off the precipice, hoping that on his way down he could break his fall by grabbing a tree he knew to be there."

Although he did not get as much out of the 1974 settlement with Israel as he had hoped, Assad continued to be optimistic about persuading the United States to side with him on the Golan Heights issue. Indeed, the return of those lands was so important to Assad that he was willing to take actions that would indirectly benefit Israel. He showed this willingness in 1976 when he sent troops into Lebanon—over the objections of the Soviet Union.

Lebanon had been declared a separate state in 1926, four years before Syria. (Lebanon gained complete independence a year before Syria did.) But in 1976, a half-century later, Lebanon was one of the most unstable countries in the world. Its main problem was that it was made up of a mixture of religious and political factions—the most serious division being that between its Christians and its Moslems. Lebanon had been on the verge of full-scale civil war. Because of its strategic location in the Middle East, Communist and Western countries had always taken an interest in Lebanon's affairs. In 1958, for example, President Dwight D. Eisenhower had sent American troops into Lebanon to support the elected government.

The trouble of 1975-76 was due to old unresolved conflicts that had been complicated by the influx of Palestinians from Jordan in 1971. More Palestinians in Lebanon meant a change in the uneasy balance of power between Christians and Moslems; they also meant greater danger for neighboring Israel. By 1972, PLO guerrillas based in southern Lebanon were regularly attacking Israeli settlements along the northern border. Israel was convinced that many Arab terrorist attacks, including the massacre of Israeli athletes at the 1972 Olympic Games in Munich, were sponsored by these Lebanese-based PLO forces. In response, Israel attacked PLO bases in Lebanon. Fighting also broke out between Lebanese Christians and the Palestinians. The uneasy peace in the Middle East seemed about to shatter.

At the invitation of the Christian president of Lebanon, Assad sent Syrian forces into that country to help quell the disturbances. While Syrian intervention helped the Lebanese Christians indirectly, by stopping the fighting, Assad, in his role as peacekeeper, did not lose face with the Palestinians. A long-time champion of Palestinian rights—and a sincere champion of those rights, as long as they did not threaten the stability of Syria—Assad took the opportunity in Lebanon to work to secure the loyalty of PLO forces there. He shared with them his plans for the first phase of his dream of Arab union: the merger of Syria, Lebanon, and Palestine (which meant both Israel and Jordan) as the heart of a united Arab nation. The plan has not yet succeeded. Eight years later, Syrian troops were still in Lebanon, and Arab unity was still a dream.

Both the United States and Israel were grateful to Assad for sending his troops into Lebanon and preventing the defeat of the Lebanese Christians. Assad hoped that in return Israel, under pressure from the United States, would pull its troops out of the rest of the Golan Heights. Assad met with President Jimmy Carter in Geneva in May 1977, and came away believing that Carter would push for a regional peace settlement that would include the return of the Golan Heights to Syria. When Israel refused to withdraw, Assad felt betrayed. He began to supply the PLO forces in Lebanon with equipment and supplies.

Assad also resented the Egyptian-Israeli talks that ended with the signing of the Camp David accords. He bitterly opposed Anwar el-Sadat's conciliatory tactics, which flew in the face of his own ideas of Arab unity.

Uprisings against the Assad government continued sporadically until early 1982, when Assad decided to take radical action against dissidents in his country. Having learned that members of the Moslem Brotherhood were trying to organize a rebellion in the city of Hama, Assad ordered his troops to begin firing on the city in February. For three weeks, the city was pounded with tank and artillery fire. Whole neighborhoods were reduced to rubble; an estimated 20,000 of the 180,000 inhabitants were killed, including scores of women, children, and innocent citizens. And all that destruction had been because perhaps 200 people in Hama belonged to the Moslem Brotherhood and had plotted against Assad. Needless to say, the message Assad wanted to send to his countrymen came through loud and clear: There was no more antigovernment activity in Syria.

Four months later, in June, Israel invaded Lebanon. Its purpose was to destroy all PLO bases there and drive out the guerrillas. In occupying the areas of Lebanon that they had seized, the Israeli forces relied on Lebanese Christian militias. (The Lebanese government was headed by a Christian.) In September, some of these militiamen massacred hundreds of Palestinian refugees in the Lebanese refugee camps of Sabra and Shatila. World opinion, which had opposed the Israeli invasion, was outraged by the massacre of innocent Palestinians. The Palestine Liberation Organization suddenly found itself viewed with sympathy, and there was a groundswell of sentiment in favor of giving the Palestinian refugees the homeland for which they had yearned and fought for almost forty years.

As a longtime supporter of the PLO and the cause of the Palestinian refugees, Assad asserted his right to be a part of any such negotiations, and there were many in the PLO who supported him. After all, he had given arms and economic aid to the PLO in the past few years and had made the Syrian-controlled areas of southern and eastern Lebanon a virtual haven for the PLO. Yasir Arafat, the leader of the PLO, did not want to give this kind of power to Assad, but he found himself outmaneuvered.

In September 1982 President Ronald Reagan proposed a plan that would provide for a Palestinian-Jordanian association. He suggested that Jordan's King Hussein represent the PLO in the necessary negotiations with Israel, since Israel refused to negotiate with the PLO. When Yasir Arafat found "some positive elements" in the Reagan plan and agreed to talk with Hussein, Assad charged Arafat with selling out the Palestinians. In protest against Arafat's plans, radical elements in the PLO rioted in the Syrian-controlled areas of Lebanon in May 1983, and for the first time in many years, Arafat's ability to control the PLO was in question.

Assad now had the upper hand in influencing the PLO. Arafat was forced to go to Damascus, the capital of Syria, to try to negotiate an end to the rebellion in his own ranks. When he would not consent to Assad's terms, Assad ordered him out of the city. Damascus had become, in effect, the headquarters of the radical PLO, and the man who claimed to be its leader was not welcome there.

Meanwhile, the civil war in Lebanon had heated up again. The Israeli government, stung by the reaction of the world and of its own people against its campaign in Lebanon, did not wish to undertake any new actions there. Other forces stepped in, however, to protect Western interests, and to "maintain the independence and integrity of Lebanon." The French, who had held the mandate over present-day Syria and Lebanon after World War I, sent peacekeeping forces; so did Italy and the United States. United States marines arrived in Lebanon in

September 1982 to help keep the peace. They were still in Lebanon in October 1983, when a United States command post was blown up by a Moslem fanatic driving a truck full of explosives. Two hundred forty-one marines were killed. That same night, a French command post was attacked in the same way, and more than fifty French troops died in the blast.

The possibilities for a real settlement among Lebanon's feuding religious and political factions seemed remote. The combatants could not even decide on a site for a meeting. The cease-fire that had been in effect since September 1982 was breaking down, with new violations every day. The tiny country was a tinderbox. Syrian forces, who had been in the country since 1976, controlled northern and eastern Lebanon. Israeli forces, in the country since June 1982, controlled much of the south. The more recently arrived United States troops were having trouble protecting themselves, to say nothing of the fragile peace.

By December 1983, Assad was very much in control in Lebanon and was in a position to influence greatly the future of the entire region. Some of his options were: to agree to a lasting cease-fire and accept the current situation—with the southern region controlled by Israel and the northern region controlled by Syria; to insist on a formal division of Lebanon into two parts; or to push for a complete Syrian takeover of Lebanon, thus reuniting the two countries. Most western experts on the Middle East agreed that, whatever happened and however it was accomplished, Syria had won and Lebanon had lost.

As far as solving the problem of the Palestinian refugees was concerned, Assad was also in the driver's seat. By December 1983, Syrian-backed PLO forces had forced Yasir Arafat and the troops loyal to him to leave Lebanon. Assad, not Arafat, was now in control of the PLO. Furthermore, United States and Israeli military analysts now say that Syria has so many modern and efficient Soviet weapons that it has surpassed Egypt as the major Arab military power.

Hafez el-Assad thus has enormous military and political power in the Middle East. How he will use this power is difficult to guess, but most experts feel he will use it to pursue his goal of a Greater Syria, which would include northern and central Lebanon and Jordan. He is beholden to the Soviet Union for much of his power, but few observers see him as a Soviet puppet. One reason he has acquired so much power is that, according to Michael Kramer in *New York* magazine, he has always had "no permanent friends, no permanent enemies, just permanent interests."

Things change quickly in the Middle East. Power bases, trouble spots, and alliances shift constantly. For now, however, Hafez el-Assad is the man to be reckoned with.

5

MENACHEM
BEGIN

Israel

Menachem Begin

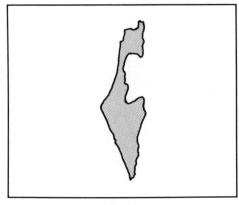

Israel

5

Israel occupies a unique position in the Middle East, indeed in
the world: It is the only country whose official religion is
Judaism. It was created out of land claimed by Arabs (the
Palestinians). Surrounded by enemies who greatly outnumber
its population and are sworn to destroy it, Israel has never in
its comparatively short existence known real peace. The object
of a full-scale attack by combined Arab forces in 1948 and again
in 1973, Israel has been subjected to almost constant terrorism
and small-scale attacks during the rest of its history. This
situation has greatly influenced its policies. Feeling very much
as if they are alone in the world, the Israelis sometimes ex-
hibit a paranoia about their country , a tendency to shoot first
and ask questions later. No Israeli leader has personified this
militant stance better than former Prime Minister Menachem
Begin, who has devoted his life to the Jewish homeland.

Begin was once the leader of the Irgun, the Jewish terrorist
organization in Palestine founded in the 1940's. In 1948, when
the first Israeli government was formed, Begin was considered
too radical to serve in that government. For many years he was
criticized for his hard-line policies, his "rigid traditions that
were intolerant and unyielding." Thus it is ironic that he was

the Israeli leader who signed a peace agreement with Egypt. On March 26, 1979, Prime Minister Begin and President Anwar el-Sadat of Egypt signed the treaty that resulted from their talks at Camp David, the presidential retreat in Maryland, the previous year. After a long and difficult series of negotiations, the two men agreed to end the thirty-year conflict between their countries. Menachem Begin thus proved to his critics that it was possible—personally and politically—to negotiate a peace that neither compromised Israel's safety nor sacrificed his life-long commitment to Zionism.

"Zion" was originally the name of the area in the ancient city of Jerusalem in which the Temple was built. Over the years Zion became synonomous with Jerusalem. When the Romans burned Jerusalem in the first century A.D., the Jews were dispersed throughout the world. Neighboring Arabs took over the land, which came to be called Palestine. For displaced Jews around the world, Jerusalem became the focal point of their yearning for a homeland. They longed to return to Zion where the Jews could be reunited as a people. In Jerusalem, in the land that their religion held to be theirs by divine order, they would be free of persecution. Zion eventually came to mean the lands of ancient Israel and, finally, Palestine. In the nineteenth century, an Austrian journalist named Theodor Herzl called for "all civilized nations to help the Jews establish a state of their own." Palestine was the suggested location of this state because of its historical and religious significance to the Jews. The movement Herzl started was called "Zionism," and it signified a return to the homeland.

Zionism grew rapidly in Poland, where Menachem Begin was born on August 16, 1913. His parents, Zev Dov Begin, a clerk in a synagogue, and Hassia Begin, were Zionists, and Menachem grew up in a household where the yearning for a Jewish homeland was strong.

At the time Menachem Begin was born, war was coming to Europe, and his parents knew that war always meant hardship for Jews. In the best of times in Europe, Jews were merely tolerated by their communities. In times of crisis, they were the targets of fierce anti-Semitism. The Begins named their third child and second son Menachem, which means "one who consoles," because it was comforting to them to bring new life into a world that would shortly be in disarray.

World War I broke out in Europe in 1914. When it reached Poland, the Begins moved to Germany, returning to Poland after the war. The persecution they suffered during the war caused them to believe even more fervently in the cause of Zionism. They were not alone.

World War I gave additional impetus to the Zionist cause in Europe and the United States. One of the treaties ending the war gave the British government authority over Palestine and hence an opportunity to implement the Balfour Declaration. The Declaration, issued in 1917 by British Foreign Secretary Lord Balfour, expressed support for the establishment of a Jewish homeland in Palestine. The Declaration also stated, however, that "nothing is to be done that might prejudice the civil and religious rights of existing non-Jewish communities." This was the only reference to the Arabs, who constituted the large majority of the people of Palestine. With the British government supporting continued Jewish immigration to Palestine, tensions there between Jews and Arabs increased and burst out in periodic acts of violence. In response, many Zionists turned to an extreme type of Zionism called Revisionism.

Founded by a Russian Jew named Vladimir Jabotinsky, Revisionist Zionism held that a Jewish state should be established at all costs, including violence if necessary. Menachem Begin's father believed in this philosophy, and the young Begin grew up steeped in Revisionist Zionist ideas. He also attended an elementary school operated by Zionists, and by the time he was ten years old, he was delivering Zionist speeches. This militant attitude aided him when, at the age of fourteen, he transferred to a Polish government school where an overwhelming majority of the students were not Jewish. In response to after-school attacks on Jewish students by non-Jews, he helped to form a "defense squad" to protect the Jewish students. Although the members of the squad were often outnumbered and badly beaten, they never gave up. In time, the bullies learned that the Jewish students were not afraid to defend themselves, and the attacks stopped.

By the time Menachem was sixteen, he was a full-fledged member of the Revisionist youth organization, Betar. Because of his fighting spirit, he rose rapidly in the organization, and while attending the University of Warsaw School of Law, he became one of Betar's nine top officers. The more responsibility Begin was given, the harder he seemed to work. While at the University, he polished his oratorical skills and used persuasive arguments to recruit new members for Betar. In less than four years he had tripled the number of Betar units in Warsaw.

Begin's ability as a dynamic speaker earned him the opportunity to give the keynote address at the Betar World Conference in Crakow in 1935. That speech drew the attention of the founder of Revisionism Vladimir Jabotinsky. After Menachem graduated from the University of Warsaw School of Law, Jabotinsky named him chief recruiter for Betar.

The major purpose of Betar—and the larger Revisionist movement—was to encourage Jews to move to Palestine to lay claim to the area. In 1933 in addition to the native Jewish population there were over 200,000 Jewish immigrants in Palestine, but that was not enough. Begin traveled all over Poland making speeches and writing manifestos, but it was difficult to get people to move from areas where they had lived for centuries. It was one thing to talk about a New Israel, it was another matter to put the ideas of Zionism into practice. Begin was frustrated by his lack of success in persuading Jews to emigrate.

The rise of Hitler in Europe helped the Zionist cause. As anti-Semitism increased during the 1930s more European Jews became willing to go to Palestine. Vladimir Jabotinsky appointed Begin as head of Betar in Poland; his duties included helping those Polish Jews who wanted to emigrate. Begin traveled throughout Poland, staying in the homes of Betar members because he lacked money for hotel accommodations. During one such trip he met his future wife, Aliza. She was nineteen and he was twenty-six, and he thought he was too old for her; but when he asked her to marry him, she accepted. They were married May 29, 1939. Both were dressed in brown Betar uniforms as they stood before the rabbi and promised to love each other until death parted them.

The threat of death was closer than they knew. Hitler's war machine was rolling across Europe. Vladimir Jabotinsky warned that Jews in Poland would not survive; he urged all European Jews to go to Palestine. Other Jewish leaders were more moderate and charged Jabotinsky with frightening European Jews. Not long afterward, Germany invaded Poland, and three million Polish Jews were caught in the Nazi invaders' net.

Jabotinsky fled to New York; the Begins escaped to Lithuania, which was under Russian political and military domination. The Russians felt that Zionism was a threat, and during the summer of 1940, the secret police began to arrest all known Zionists, including the refugees from Poland. On September 1, 1940, Begin was arrested and without being formally charged or given a trial, was sentenced to serve eight years in a Siberian labor camp. Aliza managed to avoid her husband's fate and made her way to Palestine.

Almost one year to the day after his capture, Begin was released as part of a Soviet-Polish prisoner-exchange agreement. One of the terms of the agreement was that Polish prisoners were to join the Polish Army in exile, but Begin had no intention of doing so. Within two weeks of his release, he was on his way to Palestine to join Aliza.

When Begin reached Palestine in May 1942, he was overcome with joy. He wrote later: "By the eastern bank of the Jordan River, the military convoy stopped. We rested. . . . I waded a little ways into the grass and drank in the odor of the field of my homeland. I couldn't believe I was *home*."

At the time of Begin's arrival, there were two active Revisionist organizations in Palestine—the Irgun Zvai Leumi and the Lehi. Both were made up of people who had split away from the Haganah, the secret defense arm of the official Jewish organizations in Palestine. The Haganah wanted to secure a Jewish state by peaceful negotiations and with European support. The Irgun were willing, even eager, to win an independent Jewish state by force if necessary. Both the Irgun and the Lehi were renegade and extremist, and the official Jewish organizations in Palestine advised Jews to disregard them.

In December 1943, at the age of thirty, Menachem Begin was appointed head of the Irgun. A few weeks later, he learned that

Vladimir Jabotinsky had died in the United States, his dream of a Jewish state still unrealized. Begin felt obligated to fulfill the dream of his mentor. The first step, in his opinion, was to drive the British out of Palestine. He did not have the support of official Jewish organizations, nor much support from ordinary Palestinian Jews, even though many felt they had been betrayed by the British.

Back in 1939 the British had severely curtailed Jewish immigration to Palestine; it was at a time when many Jews, fearing Hitler's rise to power, had finally decided to go to Palestine. The British explained their actions in a White Paper that stated that it was necessary to maintain a balance between Jews and Arabs in the area and that this would be impossible if the Jews fleeing from Europe were admitted. While dismayed by this British policy, official Jewish organizations went along with it, for Britain was one of Hitler's major enemies.

Begin ordered his forces to attack the British, but he did not attack the military bases in Palestine that were crucial to the Allied effort against Germany. He concentrated his forces against British establishments that dealt specifically with the government of Palestine. The attacks were well-planned and successful.

Menachem Begin became the man most wanted by the British in Palestine, and he was forced into hiding. When he learned that rumors were circulating that he had fled to the United States, he issued a declaration of revolt, calling on the Jews in Palestine to overthrow the British. The traditional Zionists ignored it, however, and the Haganah denounced the document as meaningless.

In February 1944 Begin ordered another attack on the British. Irgun forces in three cities destroyed British immigration offices and the records they contained. This made it difficult for British authorities to trace the whereabouts of Jewish immigrants and to tell which were there legally and which illegally. The British offered a $15,000 reward for information that would lead to the arrest and conviction of the Irgun leader. Begin then adopted a disguise. For several years, he presented himself as Rabbi Israel Sassover, revealing his true identity only after he was no longer wanted by the British.

Not all the Irgun actions were directed against the British; the group also attacked Palestinian Arabs. Meanwhile, Palestinian Arabs were attacking Jews. Palestine was in chaos. Eventually, the British government let the Haganah know that serious consideration was being given to their demands for a Jewish state but that the terrorism had to stop before any real progress could be made. Specifically, the British insisted that the Haganah help them curtail the activities of groups like the Irgun and Lehi.

In April 1944 David Ben-Gurion, Executive of the Jewish Agency for Palestine, launched a propaganda campaign against the Irgun and Lehi. Called "Operation Season," it was effective in persuading the majority of Jews in Palestine not to support the extremist groups. In desperation, Begin began negotiations with Lehi leaders to unite the two radical organizations, but the talks terminated when several Lehi members assassinated a British minister in Egypt. Begin insisted he knew nothing about the assassination plot, but the Irgun and Lehi were blamed equally for the act.

In 1945 World War II finally ended, and tales of the atrocities committed against Jews in European concentration camps spread throughout the world. The Zionist movement adopted the rallying cry "Never Again!" and insisted that the only way to prevent a recurrence of such horror was to allow Jews to have their own state. The majority of the members of the United Nations were moved to try to make up for what had happened to the Jews. On November 29, 1947, the UN General Assembly adopted a recommendation to partition Palestine.

Under the UN plan, Palestine was to be divided into a Jewish state, an Arab state, and a small international zone containing Jerusalem. The Palestinian Arabs would not accept the partitioning of territory they regarded as their own, and they were supported by other Arab states in the region. When, on May 14, 1948, David Ben-Gurion declared Israel a state, the Arab countries refused to recognize it as legitimate.

That same day, five Arab countries—Egypt, Syria, Lebanon, Jordan, and Iraq—declared war on Israel. Menachem Begin put political differences aside and turned over his Irgun soldiers to the Israel Defense Force command. At the Arab village of Deir

Yassin, trigger-happy Irgun soldiers opened fire on innocent civilians, resulting in the massacre of hundreds of children, women, and old men. Begin, as official leader of the Irgun, shared in the blame. Although he denied having anything to do with the tragedy, he was associated with the senseless act that shattered even the slim chance that there could be peaceful negotiations with the Palestinians.

Unlike other Zionist leaders around the world, Menachem Begin was not invited to be involved in the formation of the new government of Israel. David Ben-Gurion, who became Israel's first prime minister, believed that Begin was a "very dangerous man," and when he set up his cabinet, he included members of every political group except the Irgun and the Communists.

Begin's career was not over yet, far from it. He formed the Herut (Freedom) party and served in the first Knesset (Israeli Parliament) as the opposition leader. Over the next eighteen years, Begin pursued the course he thought was best for his young country, a course that saw him sometimes siding with Ben-Gurion and other times opposing him. When Egypt's President Nasser nationalized the Suez Canal in 1956, Begin supported Ben-Gurion's decision to help the French and British recapture it. However, when Ben-Gurion agreed to pull Israeli troops out of the Sinai Desert after UN forces took control of the canal, Begin protested loudly.

By 1966 Ben-Gurion was aging and in poor health, and many people doubted his ability to govern. By contrast, Menachem Begin had increased his power. After steadily adding to the number of seats it held in the Knesset, his Herut party had joined with the Liberal party to form a new coalition called Gahal, and Begin had become the leader of the coalition. Thus he was in a strong position to oppose his old rival. But when Levi Eshkol, second-in-command in Ben-Gurion's Labor party, declared Ben-Gurion unfit to lead and set up an emergency government, Begin was one of the first to support the prime minister and ask Eshkol to reconsider. Despite his differences with Ben-Gurion, Begin respected him and believed he had always done what he thought was best for Israel. Eshkol refused to reconsider the idea of setting up an emergency government, and Begin soon found out why.

Israeli intelligence sources had reported Arab military preparations, and the suspicion was that they were getting ready for another combined attack against Israel. Moshe Dayan, Israel's defense minister, had recommended that Israel strike first and cripple the Arab forces' ability to retaliate. Ben-Gurion had opposed the idea, and the emergency government had been formed to overrule the prime minister and take action. The new government, called the National Unity government, replaced the government of Ben-Gurion on May 2, 1967. As leader of an increasingly powerful coalition, Menachem Begin was included in the cabinet.

Begin had consistently called for Jewish occupation of the territory on both sides of the Jordan River, and he was wholeheartedly in favor of the Israeli attack that began on June 5, 1967. The war lasted six days, at the end of which Israel was victorious. Begin was overjoyed that the Six-Day War gave Israel control of the West Bank territories the Revisionists call by their ancient names—Judea and Samaria. The Old City of Jerusalem had also been taken and was now under Israeli rule. Israel had also occupied the Gaza Strip, the Sinai Peninsula, and the Golan Heights.

To the rest of the world, however, Israel had been wrong to strike first. Based on a UN charter prohibition on keeping lands gained by aggression, the United Nations Security Council passed Resolution 242, which demanded that Israel give back the lands it had aquired in the war. For Begin, the idea of giving up any of the lands won in June 1967 was unthinkable. When Golda Meir, who had become prime minister of the National Unity government in 1969, implied that she might be willing to accept the UN resolution, Begin opposed her relentlessly. Because of his hard-line attitude and the conflict with Prime Minister Meir, Begin resigned his cabinet post and returned to the Knesset as opposition leader.

Begin was not the only Israeli political leader who was opposed to giving back any of the lands seized in 1967. Israel held on to the territories and sent settlers into the areas to underscore and defend its claim. The Arab countries grew ever more bitter toward Israel over the question of the seized lands and gave aid to the PLO guerrillas, who constantly attacked the new Israeli settlements. Eventually, several Arab countries decided to try to retake the conquered lands.

On October 6, 1973, Egyptian, Syrian, and Iraqi forces launched a two-pronged attack against Israel from the west and north. It was Yom Kippur, the holiest day of the year for Jews, and the Israeli military installations in the disputed territories were undermanned. This time, Israeli military intelligence was caught completely unawares. The Israeli forces managed to organize quickly and fight back, but by the time a cease-fire was declared on October 25th, they had lost many men and much equipment. For Menachem Begin, the war was proof that Israel could never relax its vigilance. He publicly blamed Prime Minister Golda Meir for allowing the country to be caught off guard. Although Meir called for and won a vote of confidence in the Knesset, her ability to govern was seriously eroded and eventually, in June 1974, she resigned.

Yitzhak Rabin, an Israeli-born military leader and Israel's ambassador to the United States, took power. Although the Labor party was rapidly declining in popularity, Rabin was the first leader who was not a "founder," and there was hope that his administration would give the old party new life. It was not to be; scandal and corruption marked the Rabin government and destroyed the Labor party. After Rabin's administration, Begin's militance seemed easier to take, and even his severest critics could not dispute his impeccable character.

The Unity campaign platform was basically the old Revisionist doctrine. Israel's boundaries were to include all the land between the Mediterranean and the Jordan River; Israel would forever be the homeland of the Jews. Begin promised his countrymen that he would keep Israel strong militarily, and never again allow it to be caught unprepared. He also promised to encourage the growth of industry in order to make Israel more self-sufficient. In addition, his support of Israeli settlements on the West Bank, the Sinai Peninsula and the Golan Heights signalled that he had no intention of engaging in peace negotiations with any Arab state.

Begin's party emerged from the election with a bare majority. In order to secure enough votes in the Knesset to be elected prime minister and to enact his policies into law, he formed a coalition government with the Democratic Movement for Change. On the evening that he presented his new government to the Knesset, the sixty-four-year-old veteran of violence called for peace.

Not long afterward, peace, in the person of Egyptian President Anwar el-Sadat, came knocking at his door. Sadat, a long-time enemy of Israel, had ordered the Egyptian attack on the Sinai on Yom Kippur 1973. He seemed like the last person who would be willing to make peace overtures to Israel. But Sadat had lost his brother in the October War, and that loss had caused him to question the wisdom of the continuing hatred and bloodshed that plagued relations between Israel and the Arab states. Aware that he was very much alone in making any peace overtures toward Israel and that he risked incurring the hatred of other Arabs, Sadat let it be known that if Begin invited him to come to Jerusalem, he would come. Asked by the world press to respond to Sadat's initiative, Begin extended the invitation.

Sadat was the first Arab leader to visit Israel since its founding almost thirty years before, and it is interesting—and perhaps no coincidence—that his historic visit took place in November, the same month in which the UN General Assembly had voted in 1947 to partition Palestine and permit the formation of the state of Israel. The world waited to see how Begin would respond.

Begin agreed to talk with Sadat about peace, but after a while it became clear that there were certain issues on which he would not compromise. The major problem was his refusal to admit that UN Resolution 242 (passed after the Six-Day War and demanding that Israel give up the lands it had seized) applied to the West Bank, the area he had always insisted was part of the Jews' homeland by natural and eternal right. The Palestinians who were living on the West Bank were welcome to live under Israeli laws, but as long as the Palestine Liberation Organization continued its policy of violence against the state of Israel, Begin felt there could be no peace. He also refused to recognize the PLO as the legitimate spokesmen for the Palestinian people.

Begin spoke a lot about what could not be negotiated and very little about compromise. He indicated at last that the Sinai lands might be negotiable, and this small softening of his position set the stage for the peace talks at Camp David, Maryland.

Hosted by President Jimmy Carter, the talks between Begin and Sadat began on September 5,1978 and lasted for thirteen days. In the end, Begin agreed to remove Israeli settlements from the Sinai Peninsula in exchange for normal relations with Egypt. There were no provisions for giving the Palestinians a homeland, for Begin still refused to discuss that matter. He felt that he had given enough.

Back in Israel, Begin was criticized for giving away too much. The Knesset debated for hours the question of whether to approve the agreements reached at Camp David, but Begin eloquently defended his position and won the approval of the Israeli parliament. On March 26, 1979, in Washington, D.C., Begin and Sadat officially signed a peace treaty between Israel and Egypt. Less than three months earlier, on December 10, 1978, the two leaders had shared the Nobel Peace Prize for their efforts to bring peace to the Middle East. The partnership between the two men was both hopeful and ironic, for, judging from history, they were an unlikely pair to share anything but mutual hatred.

By early 1982 much had changed. Jimmy Carter was no longer President of the United States, having been defeated by Ronald Reagan in the November 1980 elections. Anwar el-Sadat had been assassinated on October 6, 1981; and Aliza Begin had died of a heart attack. Menachem Begin was in poor health and deeply depressed over the loss of his wife. Nevertheless, he held firmly to the reins of power and to the terms of the Camp David accords.

Unfortunately, an important issue had been left out of the accords—what to do about the Palestinian Arabs. As long as there was no satisfactory agreement about the Palestinians between Israel and Egypt—not to mention the other Arab countries and the PLO—whatever peace there was in the Middle East remained a fragile one. As time passed and the question remained unresolved, the tensions in the Middle East grew. The Palestine

Liberation Organization, led by Yasir Arafat, began to receive a more sympathetic hearing from non-Arab countries. Other Arab states began to band together to support the PLO and to ostracize Egypt for its treaty with Israel. Egyptian president Hosni Mubarak, who succeeded Sadat, was not as willing as his predecessor to act independently. Begin began to feel that Israel was again in danger and that the only way to act in the face of threats was aggressively.

In June 1981 Israeli war planes bombed a nuclear reactor in Iraq. Begin called the bombing "an act of salvation," charging that the Iraqis had intended to produce atomic bombs for future use against Israel and that he had acted "in the interest of national defense." During the following month, Israeli planes bombed the headquarters of the Palestine Liberation Organization in Beirut. Begin explained that the presence of the PLO in Lebanon was a threat to Israel. In December the Israeli Knesset voted to annex the Golan Heights, one of the disputed territories east of the Jordan River that Israel had occupied since 1967. President Reagan declared that this was an act of aggression and suggested that the United States punish Israel through trade sanctions. Begin blasted back: "You declare that you are punishing Israel. What kind of talk is that? 'Punishing Israel?' Are we a vassal state? A banana republic? Are we fourteen-year-old boys that if they don't behave they have their knuckles smacked?"

The Reagan administration was not quite as friendly to Israel as previous American governments. Reagan made no secret of his interest in including the Arabs in Middle East peace negotiations. His 1982 peace plan, which was based on UN Resolution 242, would have included the PLO in peace negotiations, but it would also have obtained implied recognition by Arab countries of Israel's right to exist. PLO leader Yasir Arafat called the plan "a good beginning." In Begin's opinion, the plan was a betrayal of Israel. He steadfastly refused to consider the return of the West Bank, the Golan Heights, or the establishment of a Palestinian state anywhere near Israel. He also remained firmly convinced that PLO bases near Israeli borders had to be eliminated if Israel was to survive. This is the reason why, in June

1982, Israeli forces invaded Lebanon, concentrating their attacks on areas they had identified as centers of PLO activity.

Once again world opinion turned against Israel. Some people feared that Begin really wanted to occupy more land. Begin and his defense minister, Ariel Sharon, insisted that their only mission was to destroy the PLO headquarters and drive their enemy out of Lebanon.

The Israelis were helped in their occupation of areas in southern Lebanon, by Lebanese Christian militias. More trouble followed. On September 16, 1982, Sharon allowed Christian militiamen to enter two Palestinian refugee camps, Sabra and Shatila, ostensibly to arrest the Palestinian guerrillas whom the Israelis believed remained there. Instead the militias slaughtered men, women and children.

Israeli citizens, like the people of the rest of the world, were shocked, and they protested the killing of innocent people. After a lengthy investigation, Ariel Sharon was forced to resign; as defense minister he was thought to have been aware of what might happen when the Christian militias entered the camps. Menachem Begin was also chastised for "indifference during the killings." Although no action was taken against him, his effectiveness was severely limited.

Yitzhak Navon, then President of Israel, suggested that Menachem Begin would do well to remember and heed the philosophy of David Ben-Gurion, saying: "From the beginning, Ben-Gurion believed that if Israel would be like all other nations, its chances for progressing would be minimal; that the best of Jewish youth in the free world wouldn't come unless we were special, attracting them by the challenge to help build a model society. And he knew that we would never be able to compete in numbers and in wealth with the Arabs, we had to maintain a moral and intellectual superiority."

Menachem Begin was not very much moved by quotes and references to a man whom he had opposed politically. He did not share Ben-Gurion's ideas about what Israel ought to be. He would have no quarrel with Ben-Gurion's vision if the world were different. In the real world, however, he felt that Israel had to be aggressive, strike first, and do whatever was necessary to remain alive. He felt that Israel's existence could be better protected by military superiority than by the moral and intellectual kind. By pursuing his own vision, Begin risked unpopularity in his own country and among the traditional allies of Israel; but he was used to that. In the waning years of his life and of his power, he seemed disinclined to change, and his supporters stood willing to back him up.

On August 28, 1983, Menachem Begin decided to let those others take up his fight. Saying that he was tired, he announced to his cabinet that he was resigning. He held off on sending in a formal letter of resignation until his Herut party could unite behind someone to succeed him, but he would not be talked out of resigning. Within a week, the Herut party had chosen Israeli Foreign Minister Yitzhak Shamir to replace Begin.

The importance of Shamir's policies in Israeli history is not decided. More recently, the Labor-Likud coalition succeeded the Shamir government and Shimon Peres became prime minister.

With Begin's resignation came the end of an era in the history of Israel. As Israeli President Chaim Herzog pointed out at the time, Begin's departure "brings to an end the generation of the founders. We are finished with the generation of giants."

Weary as he was, Menachem Begin probably chuckled over that statement, for there was a time when he was not included among Israel's founders, when, indeed, he was regarded by other founders as an enemy. It had taken him decades to achieve the level of popular acceptance that allowed him to become prime minister. His "era" had lasted a mere six years.

Those six years had been stormy ones. Begin was no caretaker prime minister; he was a man of action. In his time in office, he made his mark as the most militant Israeli leader in history. Ironically, he was also the Israeli leader who signed the first peace treaty with an Arab nation in Israel's history.

6

FAHD

and the

HOUSE of SAUD

Saudi Arabia

Fahd ibn Abdul Aziz al Saud

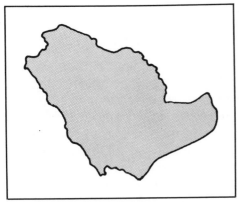
Saudi Arabia

6

Saudi Arabia is a country that carries the name of the family that rules it. The ruling family, the House of Saud, is composed of about three thousand adults and holds all the top positions in the government. It governs the country without a constitution, a parliament, or popular elections. Within the family there are various factions, but the most powerful are the ones that are direct descendants from Abdul Aziz ibn Saud, the man who unified the Arabian tribes to form the country known as Saudi Arabia.

The House of Saud maintains control over the largest country in the Middle East (with a population of 10,400,000) by paying careful attention to tradition—both religious and political—while, at the same time, taking gradual steps toward modernization. The family takes advantage of Saudi Arabia's wealth and religious importance to claim a major role in the affairs of the Middle East and to work for a unified Arab world.

Modern Saudi Arabia has its origins in the 18th century when Mohammed ibn Abd al-Wahhab launched a movement to purify Islam of all additions to its doctrine since the third century of the Muslim era. Among his most powerful converts were the Saud tribe in northeast Nejd, who began what was essentially a holy war against their neighbors in 1763. By 1811 the Wahhabis ruled all of Arabia except Yemen. In that year, however, they were defeated by an Egyptian expedition sent by the Ottoman sultan. The Wahhabis regrouped in the Nejd and in 1821 established the control of the House of Saud for a second time, primarily along the Persian Gulf of Arabia. After 1833 the Saudis saw their power steadily weakened by competing dynasties and in 1889 they were defeated by the Rashid dynasty, which gained effective control over Arabia and forced the Saudis to flee to neighboring Kuwait.

Within a decade, Abdul Aziz ibn Saud, a descendant of the first Wahhabi rulers, had undertaken the reconquest of Arabia. By 1906 he controlled the Nejd, the Saudis' traditional base of power. During World War I he took advantage of the fighting between the British and the Ottoman Empire to extend his control over other areas, and after the war, in 1924-25, he succeeded in capturing the Hijaz region, which contained the two most important cities in the history of Islam—Mecca, the birthplace of the Prophet, and Medina, the city Mohammed used as his base as he converted and conquered Arabia. By a series of agreements with Great Britain, the border between ibn Saud's territory and Transjordan was defined, and the border between ibn Saud's territory and Iraq was agreed upon by those two states. By 1932 the third Saudi kingdom had been established.

One of ibn Saud's first priorities was to establish his family and his nation as the keeper of the flame of Islam. Having captured the holy cities of Mecca and Medina, he took on the responsibility of defending and protecting these holy shrines for the 750 million Moslems the world over. As members of the Wahhabi sect, the House of Saud has taken that responsibility very seriously. Saudi Arabia and the Saud family serve as the hosts of Islam. The family spends large sums of money to keep the holy shrines in the two cities in good repair, and all roads leading to them are safe and passable for the thousands of pilgrims who pour into Mecca and Medina each year. It is one of the tenets of Islam that all Moslems must visit Mecca at least once in their lifetime. Pilgrims, who often fell prey to robbers in the past, now make their way in relative safety, thanks to strict enforcement of a Saudi law requiring public execution of anyone found guilty of harming a pilgrim.

Once ibn Saud had established in the minds of Arabs the close connection between the House of Saud and the holy shrines of Islam, he found it easier to pursue his policies in other areas of life. They included uniting Saudi Arabia under a system of centralized government, establishing a security system to protect the country's borders, and installing a communication system that would link together his large and far-flung nation. He also sought to build up his country's economy and to introduce manufacturing and organized agriculture into a land whose separate tribes had traditionally depended on the barter of livestock—camels, goats, and sheep—for the food and other items they needed to survive.

In the 1930's, ibn Saud's plans for developing the economy of Saudi Arabia received a boost the likes of which he could never have dreamed. Beneath the surface of this barren desert land with its widely separated oases, this land that has no rivers or forests and on which few crops can be made to grow, lie vast stores of the rich, dark liquid that industrial nations need in ever-increasing quantities: oil. Its discovery brought great changes.

Oil was struck in Iran, Iraq, and Bahrain and despite the efforts of British companies to suppress it, a kind of oil rush resulted. Large American and British companies applied for and received drilling rights from ibn Saud and other Middle Eastern leaders. Where they found oil, the companies paid the country royalties—a percentage of the profits—on whatever the fields produced. A few years later, the American-owned Arabian Standard Oil Company struck oil in the Dhahran area of Saudi Arabia, directly across the Persian Gulf from Bahrain. The first shipments went out in September 1938.

From then on, new oil strikes came one after the other in various parts of the Middle East, mostly in the Persian Gulf area. Iran, Iraq, the tiny country of Kuwait, and Saudi Arabia itself proved to have the largest reserves, and in the course of a very few years they became the richest countries in the Middle East. The royalties from the barrels of oil pumped from their desert lands added up to millions of dollars. The need for labor created by the oil industry caused such a wide open job market that the oil-rich countries had to import men just to keep up with the demand for labor. By the time ibn Saud died in 1953, at the age of seventy-seven, the nation he had created by unifying the various Arab tribes had come to enjoy a standard of living far beyond what he could have imagined.

Ibn Saud left hundreds of children. Four sons—Saud, Faisal, Khalid, and Fahd—have ruled the country since his death, each leaving his mark on Saudi Arabia. As the eldest son, Prince Saud succeeded to the throne, but he did not have his father's character and was not equipped to carry on ibn Saud's tradition of government. Being suddenly elevated to a position of control over unimaginable wealth was more than he could handle. It was as if he had become drunk on oil. His riotous living, extravagant spending, and misuse of authority nearly destroyed the position of his family and almost drove the country into bankruptcy. Eleven years after he assumed power, he was deposed by a group that comprised primarily his own relatives as well as assorted tribal chiefs and religious leaders.

Prince Faisal became king in 1964, and he moved easily into the position. In reality, he had been managing the government and its foreign policy during Saud's reign. Among the continuing foreign policy problems were sharp disagreements with Egypt and the other Arab countries that did not have oil. These disputes had started in the 1930's, soon after the first big oil strike. The basis of their hostility at all times was jealousy, but by the 1950's, Egypt and the others had learned to present their charges in the guise of resentment against Israel. Their anger was directed not only at Saudi Arabia but at the British and Americans, who— to their minds—had forced the establishment of Israel and were drilling oil in Arab lands and making enormous profits. In the late 1950's, Egypt's President Nasser denounced British and American "colonialism" in Arabia and sent troops to occupy Yemen, a small country to the south of Saudi Arabia.

The House of Saud had not supported the establishment of Israel, and Prince Faisal deeply resented Nasser's insinuations. In fact, he felt that Nasser had insulted both his family and his country. Moreover, he did not approve of the Egyptian move into Yemen, whose monarchy he supported. He and Nasser became bitter enemies and remained so for close to a decade, even after he became king.

Then, in June 1967, Israel responded to reports by its military intelligence that some of its Arab neighbors were planning another assault on it. Israeli bombers attacked airfields in Jordan and Egypt, and in the space of six days managed to take Syria's Golan Heights, Jordan's West Bank, Arab Jerusalem, and the entire Sinai Peninsula. The attack so devastated the Arab states involved that all Arabs shared in the humiliation. Faisal waited for Nasser to come to him for help, and when the Egyptian president was forced to seek aid from his enemy, Faisal insisted that Egypt withdraw its troops from Yemen. Once that was accomplished, Saudi Arabia gave Egypt and the other Arab states that had suffered the Israeli attack millions of dollars in aid to rebuild their armed forces. When Nasser died suddenly in September 1970 and Anwar el-Sadat succeeded him as president of Egypt, Faisal willingly extended even more aid to that country.

It was not just a sense of Arab nationalism that moved Faisal to help the Egyptians; deeply-held religious beliefs also played a part. He wanted Jerusalem, considered the third most holy city in Islam, to be in Arab hands. He swore that before he died he would pray in al-Aqsa Mosque, in the Israeli-occupied part of Jerusalem, even if it meant war. He realized that Saudi Arabia did not have to wage this war itself in order to recapture Jerusalem. Saudi Arabia had a stronger weapon than any tank or airplane; it controlled the oil that kept the war machines running.

When Anwar el-Sadat confided that he wanted to attack Israel and avenge the humiliation of the Six-Day War, Faisal was more than willing to provide financial support. Over the next five years he raised some $200 million with which the Egyptians purchased arms from the Soviet Union. He also pledged to supply Egypt with all the oil it needed. Thus when, in October 1973, Egyptian forces attacked Israel and crossed the Suez Canal in an attempt to recapture the Sinai Peninsula, the pride in this show of force belonged to the Saudis as well as to the Egyptians.

Other Arab countries considered the victory theirs, too. That same year, oil-rich countries founded OPEC (the Organization of Petroleum Exporting Countries), and in a display of economic might, they raised the price of oil from $3.01 to $5.12 per barrel. Faisal opposed this move. He sent a personal letter to United States President Richard Nixon suggesting that if the United States halted its shipments of arms to Israel, the OPEC countries might be persuaded to reconsider the price increase. Nixon denied the request and instead ordered the massive reinforcement of Israel. Angered, Faisal ordered a halt to all oil shipments to the United States. Other OPEC countries joined in; only Libya and Iraq did not participate.

The Western economies went into a skid as oil prices suddenly rose to between $12 and $17 a barrel. Suddenly, peace in the Middle East became a grave concern to the West. The foreign ministers of the European Economic Community called on Israel to end its occupation of the territories it had captured in 1967. There was talk of the rights of the Palestinians. This sudden interest in the political and social problems of the area was really just a mask for the concern about the oil supply and what the combination of increased prices and the embargo against the United States would do to the world economy. Secretary of State Henry Kissinger visited Faisal, the first time an American secretary of state had visited the kingdom in twenty-six years. But Faisal's requirements for lifting the embargo were too stiff: Israeli withdrawal and the restoration to the Palestinians of their rightful homeland.

Arab solidarity was never more evident than at this time. In February 1974, Faisal convened a pan-Islamic conference in Cairo, which was attended by representatives from nearly every Islamic country. At the conference the PLO, represented by Yasir Arafat, was raised from observer status to full membership. The many conflicts among the Islamic countries were put aside in a spirit of unity, and countries shared in the sense of "the importance of the Arab world for the welfare of the world economy."

Meanwhile, the United States had continued to pursue the friendship of the Saudis and agreed to sell modern tanks, naval vessels, and fighter aircraft to Saudi Arabia. Secretary of State Kissinger also promised American technicians to transform

Saudi Arabia's oil dollars into industries, roads, railways, air-
ports, schools, and hospitals. Faisal lifted the oil embargo and
opened the floodgates to an unprecedented rush of development. Buildings went up everywhere, car imports tripled in just
one year, consumer goods of all kinds poured into the country.
Saudi Arabia was modernizing with dizzying speed.

Faisal was dismayed by these developments. He worried that
the simple pieties of Islam would be overcome by greed and
affluence. He worried that he had betrayed his people. He grew
sad and depressed and distant from his family. He began to have
dreams that he thought foretold his death. On March 25, 1975,
he was assassinated by a nephew whose life had borne out the
old king's worst fears. The nephew, Faisal ibn Musad Abdul
Aziz had been in and out of several colleges in the United States,
had been caught with LSD, and had behaved so irresponsibly
that when he had returned home the king had decreed that he
remain in the country. Faisal ibn Musad Abdul Aziz had a
history of erratic behavior; he also had a grudge against King
Faisal because of the execution of his older brother ten years
before after an attack on a Riyadh TV station. Nevertheless, the
real reasons why he killed his uncle remain unclear. What is
clear is that by his act he ended an era for Saudi Arabia, one in
which the country had begun to change into a modern state and
to be a major power in the world.

Khalid ibn Abdul Aziz al Saud, who had been crown prince
under Faisal, succeeded to the throne within an hour of his
brother's death. Born in Riyadh in 1913, Khalid was reared in
the tradition of a desert prince. He attended Islamic schools and
was drilled in Koranic law and the legal code of the Wahhabi
sect. His interests then were not in politics and power; he preferred instead to hunt and to race camels. He agreed only reluctantly to become crown prince, and did it primarily because
he adored his older half brother. With Faisal's guidance he
learned how to govern, and he represented the Saudi government
at several international conferences, but most observers felt
that Khalid did not have the flair, or charisma, or ambition, to
be a great king. Perhaps the family, too, felt this way, for they
did not follow the customary line of succession in choosing a

crown prince for Khalid. The two brothers who were next in line in age were bypassed in favor of Prince Fahd, Khalid's fifty-two-year-old half brother.

The new crown prince was born in 1922. His mother was the favorite wife of Abdul Aziz ibn Saud, and her clan was among the most influential in Arabia. Fahd was educated at home and in Islamic schools and after graduation from high school attended universities in Europe and the United States. He was aggressive, ambitious, and forceful, and it was felt that he would be the real power behind the throne.

It was Fahd who delivered the first policy statement of the Khalid administration. Speaking on behalf of King Khalid, the crown prince assured the Saudis that modernization programs and social reform would continue. He emphasized that the Saudis wanted to play a major role in settling regional disputes and warned that the king was steadfast in his support of the Palestinian people's rights to a homeland. But the crown prince did not deliver many more speeches in King Khalid's place. The role of king grew on Khalid, and during the seven years of his reign he proved a strong leader in all areas of government.

Khalid continued King Faisal's internal development program by implementing a five-year plan that cost $250 billion. Education, medical care, and housing particularly interested him, and he channeled millions of dollars into improving conditions in those areas. He insisted on good work in those improvements. He was once taken to see a low-rent housing development that was being built and was dismayed to see what he called "match boxes." He declared that no one should have to live in such housing, and the project was abandoned.

In international affairs, Khalid upheld Arab causes and worked to normalize relations with the United States, although he was more cautious than the crown prince would have wanted. Khalid was not nearly as opposed to Israel as Faisal had been; but he insisted, as Faisal had, that Middle East peace required the withdrawal of Israel from all territories occupied in the 1967 war—including the Old City of Jerusalem—and that the Palestinians must have a homeland. Still, both President Jimmy Carter of the United States and President Anwar el-Sadat of

Egypt hoped that the Saudis would cooperate in Sadat's Middle East peace initiative.

Sadat visited Riyadh in October 1977, the week before his historic trip to Jeruslaem, and discussed the possibility of a joint effort for peace. The Saudis refused to commit themselves. When seven days later, Sadat, by permission of the Israelis, prayed in the al-Aqsa Mosque in Jerusalem without having given the Saudis advance notice, they felt both embarrassed and betrayed. Egypt was Saudi Arabia's major ally, and neighboring Arab countries naturally assumed that the Saudis knew about and condoned Sadat's action.

Praying in the al-Aqsa Mosque was the one thing that King Faisal had sworn he would never do as long as the city of Jerusalem was in Israel's hands. As keepers of Islam's holy places, the Saudis could not defend Sadat. As much as they might have wished to participate in Sadat's program for peace, they could not do so now that Sadat had, in their eyes, betrayed Islam. This infuriated Sadat, who called the Saudis "dwarfs standing in a pile of money." When Sadat signed the Camp David accords with Israel, Khalid broke with his old ally and led Arab sanctions against Egypt.

During his reign, Khalid was called upon to defend both the Saudi position as host of Islam and the very holy places that Saudi Arabia protected. On November 20, 1979, seven hundred armed religious militants, who had been influenced by the Ayatollah Khomeini's Shiite revolution in Iran, seized Mecca's Grand Mosque—the holiest of all Islamic shrines. Khalid first sought to make sure that sending troops to recapture the mosque would not defile the holy place and on being advised by scholars of the Koran that it would not, ordered his troops to take the mosque. This they did, in a bloody battle in which 244 people—militants and Saudi soldiers—died. Khalid was emotionally shaken by the event, and he openly cried when he visited his wounded troops. Every soldier who had participated in the battle received a personal gift from the king—a color television, a car, a gold watch. On January 9, 1980, sixty-three of the leaders of the takeover were beheaded in the public squares of eight Saudi cities.

Muammar el-Qaddafi of Libya cited the mosque takeover as proof that the Saudis could no longer be relied on as protectors of the holy shrines of Islam. He called on Moslems not to go on pilgrimages in 1980, but no one paid much attention to him. All he succeeded in doing was offending Khalid, who, in a rare display of emotion, called Qaddafi "a criminal . . . an atheist . . . a madman, [who] is facing his final days."

If his health had been better, Khalid might have proved to be an exceptional Saudi king, but he had a long history of heart disease and had undergone open heart surgery in the United States in 1972 and 1978. On June 13, 1982, while on vacation, he suffered a heart attack and died.

Crown Prince Fahd succeeded to the throne. His half brother Abdullah, commander of the National Guard, was named crown prince. It is believed that Fahd was closest to his full brother, Prince Sultan, but Khalid had stated that on his death, Abdullah should become the crown prince. The choice of the crown prince has often been a means of stabilizing family relations—by distributing power among the various factions in the family. Khalid had been selected by Faisal for this reason—and the appointment of Abdullah was made to prevent the jealousy that might have arisen if full brothers had been named to the top two positions in the government. Also, succession generally follows the order of seniority, and Abdullah is older than Sultan. Abdullah is not as pro-Western as Fahd and serves to check Fahd's strong ties with America and to reassure his Arab neighbors.

King Fahd came to the throne after many years in Saudi government. His political career began in 1953, when, as his country's first minister of education, he played a major role in building up the educational system of the country. In 1962 he became minister of the interior; his mission, as he defined it, was to maintain the "security and stability that Saudi Arabia has always enjoyed while promoting the welfare of Saudi citizens."

As crown prince, Fahd had been interested in Middle East peace initiatives and in August 1981 had issued an eight-point plan for peace that came to be called the Fahd Plan. It called for Israeli withdrawal from all territory that had been occupied since the 1967 war; removal of Israeli settlements on the West

Bank and in other occupied areas; guaranteed freedom of worship for all religious groups within these areas; recognition of the rights of the two million Palestinian refugees to repatriation or compensation; UN trusteeship over the West Bank and Gaza during a transition period of several months; establishment of an independent Palestinian state with the Arab eastern section of Jerusalem as its capital; and agreement, to be guaranteed by the United Nations, to assure the rights of all states in the area to live peacefully with each other.

This last point was especially significant, for it implied a recognition of Israel. Fahd was realistic in accepting the fact that Israel was in the Middle East to stay. He was careful not to mention Israel by name, but hard-line Arab nations understood the implications and bitterly rejected the proposal. The PLO rejected it because it recognized Israel's right to exist. Sadat called the plan "nothing new." (The Israelis also rejected the plan—having agreed to return the Sinai Peninsula to Egypt, they did not want to give up other occupied lands.) Disagreement over the Fahd Plan led to the collapse of the Arab summit meeting at Fez, Morocco, in November 1981.

Political analysts believe that the Fahd Plan was the result of a rivalry between the Saudis and Egypt over which country should be the leader of the Arab nations; but that rivalry has weakened since Fahd issued his proposals. President Hosni Mubarak, who succeeded Sadat in Egypt, attended King Khalid's funeral, and it is no secret that King Fahd is anxious to bring Egypt, which acted very independently under Sadat, back into line with the rest of the Arab world.

While Fahd continues to hope for peace in the Middle East, he has made no major new proposals since 1981. In fact, after Israel invaded Lebanon in 1982, it became politically difficult for Fahd even to imply the need for Arab recognition of Israel. After the massacre of the Palestinians in Lebanon, Fahd called for nothing less than total Israeli withdrawal from Lebanon, as well as the resignations of Prime Minister Menachem Begin and Defense Minister Ariel Sharon for their involvement in the massacre.

Under Fahd, Saudi Arabia has maintained good relationships with the United States, whose military arms and technical expertise he feels his country needs; but he has found it difficult to continue this stance when America continues to support Israel. He walks a thin tightrope, trying to maintain Saudi Arabia's power in the Arab world while continuing to deal with the West. Thus far, he has managed to keep his balance. In the fall of 1982, President Reagan agreed to sell the Saudis five airborne warning and control system planes (AWACs) on the condition that the Saudis use them only to guarantee their own security and stability, not offensively. This agreement was considered a major victory for Fahd.

Implied in the agreement was that Fahd would not use the AWACs against Israel, and Fahd has no problem with that restriction. He does not consider Israel the biggest threat to his government. When he succeeded to the throne, a French reporter asked him what he thought his major problem would be and he replied, "Fanaticism." Of major concern to Fahd and the House of Saud is Iran's threat to export its fundamentalist revolution to neighboring Persian Gulf States. This is a headache for all Arab leaders, but the Saudis are extremely troubled because of their policy of keeping their borders open, to accommodate pilgrim travel. The Saud family fears that what happened to the shah in Iran could also happen to them; and there are disturbing parallels.

Iran was an absolute monarchy; so is Saudi Arabia. Fahd will not even consider popular elections. He cites the time, a few years back, when elections were tried on the local level; rich businessmen who bought votes were the ones who were elected, he charged.

Iran was a developing country trying to advance from the fifteenth to the twentieth century in a few short years. Saudi Arabia is also like that. Money is so abundant that the Saudis have to go elsewhere to spend it. To counter the impression that Saudis are wealthy squanderers of money, Fahd increased Saudi foreign aid by twenty percent in 1983 and decreed that the money be distributed to countries in order of need.

Iran was pro-western, and so is Fahd. He enjoys the luxury his money affords him, reads and speaks English fluently, and has tried to introduce some western ways into his country. He does not live the austere, pure life insisted on by the Wahhabi sect his father worked and fought so hard for, although he does pay lip service to it. Islamic fundamentalists in his own country, in addition to those in Iran, are bitterly opposed to him.

King Fahd and the House of Saud are watching the situation in Iran closely and are prepared to act swiftly at the first signs of unrest at home. There is so much instability in the Middle East over so many things that it will become harder for King Fahd and his successors to govern their huge country—harder than it has been for anyone since Abdul Aziz ibn Saud, who founded both the country and the dynasty that has controlled it ever since. How long the House of Saud stands will depend upon how long the land remains productive, how long the people remain content, and how long its leaders can hold religious militants at bay.

7

HUSSEIN

IBN TALAL

Jordan

Hussein ibn Talal

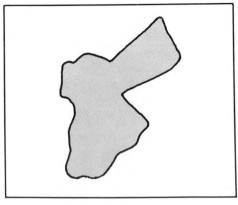

Jordan

7

On July 20, 1951, Prince Hussein of Jordan, then sixteen years old, stood beside his aging grandfather, King Abdullah, just outside the al-Aqsa Mosque in the old city of Jerusalem. Suddenly, an assassin's bullets struck the king in the head, chest, and shoulder, killing him instantly. One of the bullets is believed to have glanced off the medal Prince Hussein wore on his chest. Shouts of horror and cries of mourning resounded throughout Jordan when the news of Abdullah's assassination was reported, for he had been a prominent Middle Eastern leader for over twenty-eight years and the first king of independent Jordan.

Who would succeed him? It was common knowledge that Talal, Abdullah's son, was not well mentally, and Hussein, the next in line of succession was, at age sixteen, still a boy. Jordan had been an independent nation for only a few years, and Abdullah's death was a serious blow to hopes for the growth and stability of the country.

One of the keys to stability in Jordan was an orderly succession for its rulers, and thus the young prince was chosen to lead his country, despite his age. After a brief interim rule by a three-man council, Prince Hussein was proclaimed King of the Hashemite Kingdom of Jordan. He was crowned on May 2, 1953, his eighteenth birthday.

Politicians of the day dismissed Hussein's kingship as one that "wouldn't make a difference," especially in a world where monarchies were tumbling one after the other. There were predictions that internal strife would bring about Hussein's fall and ultimately that of Jordan. The best predictions for the reign of the teenage king were that he would become a puppet ruler, with someone else behind the scenes dictating policy. These observers were wrong, however. Though young in years, the new king had the tenacity, emotional maturity, and confidence to rise to the challenges of his position. More than thirty years later, even Hussein's severest critics recognize the king of Jordan as his own man, a leader who enjoys great influence at home and abroad. As a devout Moslem, Hussein gives Allah praise for all his success. Next, he credits his grandfather, King Abdullah, for giving him the early training that was so important to him when he was called upon to assume the leadership of his country.

A direct descendant of the Prophet Mohammed, Hussein ibn Talal was the oldest of four children born to Prince Talal and Princess Zein. Almost from birth, he was a special favorite of his grandfather. "Come always to me," the aging king said to the prince. "Try to learn from what you witness." Hussein took every opportunity to be in the king's company. Sitting at Abdullah's side while he held informal court in the palace at Raghadan, Hussein learned a great deal about how to govern a people with diverse ideas, needs, and lifestyles.

At this court Abdullah received Jordanians of all kinds—farmers from the valley region, Bedouins from the desert, Palestinians living on the west bank of the Jordan River. Thus Hussein was exposed to the many cultures within Jordan. Through firsthand contact with them, he grew to respect the people of his country, and no doubt his familiarity with the land and people contributed to his later confidence as king.

King Abdullah also shared with his grandson his pride in the family heritage and often related his own experiences. Some of these were accounts of his father, Hussein ibn Ali, Sharif of Mecca, who had been a leader in the historic Arab Awakening during World War I. Abdullah was proud, too, of his ethnic heritage and encouraged Hussein to study Arab art, poetry, architecture, and history. Most important, in Hussein's eyes, was the strong religious faith instilled in him by his grandfather, for it is his own deep faith that he feels has been the key to his successful leadership.

At the insistence of his grandfather, Hussein received a first-rate education. Beginning his studies at the age of five at the National School, he was enrolled at the Islamic Educational College in Alexandria, Egypt, when Abdullah was assassinated. Plans for Hussein's succession to the throne included his finishing his education first. He completed secondary school at Harrow in England, and although he was proclaimed king by the Jordanian parliament in August 1952, he then graduated from Victoria College in Alexandria and completed two terms at Sandhurst Military Academy in England. Thereafter, he became an officer in the Arab Legion, Jordan's army. Meanwhile, the three-man Royal Council, which had taken over from Hussein's father after he was declared mentally incompetent, continued to govern.

On May 2, 1953, nine months after he was proclaimed king, Hussein was at last crowned in the capital city of Amman. *Newsweek* described the coronation as a colorful ceremony, a "melding of the old and the new." The young king was dressed in the blue and gold uniform of an Arab Legion officer. Armored cars, jeeps, and mounted Lancers of the Arab Legion escorted him in a spectacular parade. There were 101-gun salutes in Amman and Jerusalem. Hussein presided over the ceremonies in his honor with a dignity that belied his years; but there was a lot more to being king of Jordan than appearing at public functions. The kingdom was in sorry shape and, in historic time, not much older than its teenage king.

The land we now know as Jordan has been called by many names and ruled by many groups. In the time of Moses, Jordan was known as Moab and Edom. Later on, the land became part of ancient Israel. Down through history, the borders of Jordan have expanded and contracted to include or exclude territories claimed by a long succession of foreign conquerors. Meanwhile, the nomadic Bedouins of the area lived on the land, herded their flocks, practiced their own customs and laws, and raided each other's camps as they had always done. From time to time, they joined forces to fight a common enemy and paid little attention to the boundaries set by their would-be rulers.

By 1900, the Ottoman Turks dominated the region occupied by the countries known today as Syria, Iraq, Lebanon, Jordan and Israel. During World War I, the Turks were defeated, and as part of the agreements that ended the war, the British took control of Palestine and Transjordan—now the countries of Israel and Jordan. Abdullah ibn-Husein, brother of King Faisal of Iraq, was made emir of Transjordan, which was administered separately from Palestine. Abdullah cooperated fully with the British during World War II, and Transjordan became completely independent in 1946.

The following year the United Nations voted to partition Palestine into a Jewish and an Arab state. Transjordan's army was one of the five Arab forces that answered the UN vote with an attack on the lands set aside for Israel. Though beaten back by Israel, the Transjordanians did occupy areas of Palestine that had been set aside as Arab land, and when the Arab leaders refused the land earmarked for the Palestinians Transjordan stepped in and annexed it. In 1949 the name of Transjordan was changed to Jordan to reflect the fact that it now included lands west of the Jordan River. The official name of the country became the Hashemite Kingdom of Jordan, which refers to the clan of Hashim, from which the Prophet Mohammed's family name was derived. For centuries, the House of Hashim has held a special status throughout Islam.

Israel and Jordan signed a truce and established a tentative peace in April 1949, which led some Arab leaders to criticize Abdullah for being an opportunist. The Palestinians in Jordan, to whom Abdullah offered full Jordanian citizenship, felt his move was a kind of betrayal. They wanted their own country back, and the presence in Jordan of 450,000 resentful Palestinians was hardly a condition for internal peace.

Thus, when King Hussein took power at the age of eighteen, his country had been independent for only seven years, had been known as the Hashemite Kingdom of Jordan for only four years, and had included areas that were formerly part of Palestine for only three years. Three fifths of the land was arid desert. Jordan lacked the rich oil deposits and industrial raw materials that other Arab countries enjoyed. Poor roads made transportation and communication almost impossible. Aqaba, Jordan's one port, was practically inaccessible, and a large percentage of the population suffered from poverty and lack of education.

In 1955 Hussein married Princess Dina, daughter of Abdul Hamid el-Aoun of Saudi Arabia, but after two years and two children, they were divorced. Hussein was not to enjoy a stable family life for some years. In fact, instability of all kinds plagued the early years of his reign. There were constant border clashes between Palestinian guerrillas based in Jordan and the Israelis. Israeli raids on Jordanian border towns caused Hussein to warn that unless Israel ended its aggressions, Jordan would be "compelled to reconsider the truce arranged between the two countries in 1949." In May 1955, representatives of Jordan and Israel agreed to accord prisoner of war status to soldiers or policemen captured during border clashes.

Internal peace was equally elusive. The Palestinians were dissatisfied with King Hussein's position regarding their plight. Factions within his own government disagreed with his moderate stance toward Israel and threatened to rebel. A more serious charge was that he was a puppet of the British and the Americans and did not really have the Palestinian cause at heart.

That particular criticism was hard to rebut, for Jordan relied heavily on British military support. Although Jordan was independent, by the terms of an agreement signed in 1948, Britain gave Jordan an annual military subsidy. The head of the military was Sir John Bagot Glubb, a British officer who had served in the country since 1939 and was a personal friend of the king. Hussein finally decided, however, that as long as Glubb remained commander of the Jordanian Army, Hussein's accusers could legitimately complain about British interference in Jordanian affairs. In March 1956 Hussein risked the stability of the army, and of Jordan, by dismissing Glubb and forfeiting British military aid.

He needn't have worried. With aid from other Arab nations— and from the United States—Hussein was able to upgrade the Jordanian armed forces. His training at Sandhurst Military

Academy enabled him to set an example to his troops. He learned to fly every type of plane and made a point of inspecting and learning how to operate every piece of military equipment acquired by his troops. It was not uncommon for him to fight alongside his men in battle; in a seven-hour fight that raged around the Jordanian border town of Qalqiliya in October 1956, the king spent from midnight to daybreak at an artillery post, exchanging fire with the Israeli batteries.

The propaganda campaign against Hussein continued. Hussein believed that Gamal Abdel Nasser, president of Egypt, was behind the attacks. Egypt, having turned against the West, was seeking money, weapons, and technical assistance from the Soviet Union, which, in turn, was trying to develop a communist Middle East. They hoped to use the Israel situation to plant seeds of hatred and mistrust and to persuade the militarily inferior Arab nations to turn to the Soviet Union for arms and military advisers.

Hussein rejected communist doctrines because they were not compatible with Islam: In communism, all obedience is owed to the State; in Islam, it is owed to Allah. Hussein also rejected the idea that the only way to achieve peace in the Middle East was to destroy Israel. Arabs and Jews had once lived in peace in the Middle East; he believed they could do so again. He also did not see how the Palestinians could gain their homeland if the fighting continued. He held to his moderate views even though they grew increasingly unpopular.

On April 13, 1957, fighting broke out at an army base at Az-Zarqa, thirty miles north of Amman. Hussein rushed to the base to restore order, thereby playing into the hands of a group in his government who wanted to overthrow him and set up a left-wing regime. The plotters expected that Hussein would be killed in the course of the rebellion, but they underestimated the army troops—made up largely of Bedouins, who were intensely loyal to the House of Hashim. When Hussein stood up in his car and dared any disloyal man to kill him, no one shot. Having put down the revolt, he returned to Amman to confront its leaders.

Less than a year later, another plot against Hussein was discovered. This time the king demanded oaths of allegiance to himself and Jordan from seven hundred army officers and ordered the arrest of those he believed to be disloyal. Still in his early twenties, he had forced even his enemies to respect his bravery.

While contending with internal strife and border clashes with the Israelis, Hussein devoted as much attention as he could to improving Jordan's position in the world and the quality of life of its people. Jordan gained admission to the United Nations in 1955 and was thus able to receive United Nations aid and to enjoy more favorable trade agreements. Hussein signed a multilateral trade agreement with other Arab states and ordered that Jordan's one port, Aqaba, be made more accessible so that Jordan could increase its foreign trade. He visited the United States to speak with President Eisenhower and Rome to speak with Pope John XXIII. With assistance from the United States and from other Arab countries, he planned and developed communications systems, roads, and dams. He signed new labor laws. He urged the Bedouins to give up their nomadic ways and settle in towns so that their children could go to school.

In 1961 Hussein married Antoinette Gardiner, daughter of a British colonel. After their marriage, she assumed the name of Muna el-Hussein. They had three children, including twin girls born in 1968. Also in the early 1960's, Hussein took additional steps to stabilize his country. He established a seven-year program of economic growth that included massive building programs, plans to increase productivity, and the development of Jordan's tourist industry. He also enacted an income tax to help finance many of these projects and to make Jordan less dependent on foreign aid. He started social security and health insurance programs. He developed highways and public transportation—and airlines to service the resorts that were being built. Work on the Ibn Hasna Dam was started; when completed, it would store irrigation water for the arid lands, and its hydroelectric plant would provide electricity for a large area.

Hussein knew, however, that all the economic and social progress would not solve the basic problem of what to do with the Palestinians. While almost half a million of them enjoyed full Jordanian citizenship, with the right to own land and hold government positions, they wanted their own homeland. The

Palestinians in Jordan, as well as the Palestinians elsewhere in the world, looked to Jordan and the other Arab states to redress their grievances. The passing years did not dampen their fervor; in fact, they became more impatient. Since they made up nearly ten percent of Jordan's population, they could not be ignored. By 1964, the situation was so tense that Hussein decided it was in his best interests, and Jordan's, to reconcile his differences with President Nasser of Egypt. In January of that year, he attended the Arab summit conference in Cairo, where he talked with Nasser. In August he returned to Egypt to continue their discussion of the Palestinian problem. In the same year, also under Nasser's guidance, the Palestine Liberation Organization— a loose confederation of several Palestinian rebel groups—was formed. It was headquartered in Jordan.

During this period, the mid-1960's, the Arabs were making a concerted effort to cooperate with one another and to present a united front. Hussein saw the potential in this effort and worked on its behalf. In the fall of 1964, he attended another Arab summit conference in Alexandria, and the nonaligned nations' summit conference in Cairo. In 1965 he signed the Arab Common Market agreement; in May 1967 he signed a mutual defense agreement with Egypt.

In June 1967, acting on the suspicion that Arab countries were planning an invasion, Israeli forces launched surprise attacks on Egypt, Syria, and Jordan. "It is too painful to relive," said Hussein later. "But, if I meant what I had said about Arab unity, I had no choice but to join my brothers in resisting Israeli aggression, although I was sure defeat was inevitable." Defeat came very quickly; Hussein's tourist industry and seven-year plan—and, indeed, his entire country—were in shambles. Israel had captured the West Bank and the Golan Heights, which some Israelis claimed belonged historically to Israel. The Arab section of Jerusalem had also been captured. The Palestine Liberation Organization forces in Jordan had been hit hard.

Ironically, despite the loss of life, the Six-Day War proved to be a boon for the PLO. Not only did the organization gain sympathy and recognition from the outside world, it also gained many new converts. Until that time, the majority of the Palestinian people had not supported the PLO; within days after the war, its membership had tripled. With new fighters and with a new surge of nationalism, PLO guerrillas, using Jordan as their base, continued their attacks on Israel, ignoring UN cease-fire orders.

Hussein appealed to the PLO to stop the attacks, but found he was faced with another internal conflict. Thousands of heavily-armed Palestinian guerrillas were in Jordan; he could no longer control them. Members of the PLO confronted Hussein and boldly disregarded agreements requiring them to stay in the Jordan valley and not to carry weapons in towns. Yasir Arafat's men defiantly roamed through the streets of Amman fully armed, entering houses and hotels to collect contributions for their cause. Civil war was imminent; something had to be done to stop it.

In September 1970 Hussein ordered the Jordanian army to move against the guerrillas. By July 1971 they had destroyed most of the guerrilla bases, and with a final, massive assault, they drove the PLO out of Jordan. The members of the PLO who were not killed were captured and deported or imprisoned. To the Palestinians who had not taken part in the fighting, Hussein promised that life would go on as before. He still wanted them to have their own homeland, but he stood firm in his conviction that the way to obtain that objective was through negotiation and not by force.

Meanwhile, Hussein was trying to get back the lands he had lost to Israel in the Six-Day War. He was also deeply involved in the Arab counteroffensive negotiations that led to UN Resolution 242. This called for Israel to withdraw from the occupied lands and recognized the territorial integrity and independence of all Middle East states, including Israel. Although Hussein was able to persuade the other Arab leaders to support the resolution, it proved to be ineffective because the PLO refused to support it; the PLO would not support any statement that implied that Israel had a right to exist.

The 1970's were another decade of unrest and border fighting. Hussein continued to seek peace when and where he could, while holding fast to his conviction that negotiation was the only path to permanent peace. In 1972 he proposed a United

Arab Kingdom that provided for the creation of a federal union of Palestine (Israeli-occupied territory in the West Bank and Gaza) and Jordan after the West Bank was regained, but other Arab leaders denounced him as a western stooge. Although he supplied troops and equipment to assist Syrian forces in the 1973 October War against Israel, most of his efforts were directed toward peace. He made trips to the United States and, in 1974, welcomed American President Richard Nixon to Jordan. He continued to attend Arab conferences and visited various Arab capitals.

In 1972 he divorced his wife Muna and married Alia Toukan. Their daughter was born in 1974 and their son in 1975. In 1977 Princess Alia was killed in a helicopter crash, and Hussein went into a deep depression. Soon, however, he compensated for his loss by working harder than ever. He plunged into the rebuilding of the areas of his country that had been decimated by fighting and continued the building and modernization plans he had begun during the preceding decade. He pursued the cause of Middle East peace most energetically of all. Thus he was understandably disturbed when he was not invited to participate in the talks between Israel and Egypt that resulted in the signing of the Camp David accords.

Hussein had visited President Sadat in Alexandria in 1974, and among the topics of discussion had been peace in the Middle East. He had seen Sadat at the various Arab summit meetings. Although he admitted that he probably would have refused to participate in the talks with Israel and Egypt, he felt that he should at least have been asked. The Palestinians had been Jordan's problem since 1952, and he was sure that if anyone knew their concerns and problems, he did.

Every Arab leader, other than Sadat, rejected the Camp David accords, Hussein among them. He felt that there had not been enough provision made for the Palestinians. Relations between Jordan and the United States had been good for several years, but now they became strained. When Hussein requested arms from the United States in an effort to protect Jordan's borders, he was turned down. Israel had argued against the sale. Hussein then turned to the Soviet Union, which was pleased to have the opportunity to gain a foothold in Jordan. Hussein got his arms and made his point to the Americans that he did not need them in order to survive; but he had no intention of becoming a Soviet puppet.

Hussein continued to display a moderation that was welcomed by the United States, and in 1982, when President Reagan decided to propose his own Middle East peace plan, Hussein was an important part of it. Under Reagan's plan, Jordan and the Palestinians would be part of a federal union (just as Hussein had suggested a decade earlier). Hussein was willing to consider the plan, and to talk with PLO leader Yasir Arafat about a combined Jordanian-Palestinian state. Arafat himself called the plan "positive" in some respects and agreed to talk with Hussein, even though he was still bitter about the expulsion of PLO guerrillas from Jordan in 1970 and 1971. The talks soon broke down, not so much because Arafat and Hussein could not come to an understanding, but because Arafat was having trouble keeping control of the PLO. In April Jordan rejected the Reagan peace plan, blaming the PLO. Soon afterward, in May 1983, open rebellion broke out among PLO factions in Syria.

Hussein's dream of peace in the Middle East is still no closer to becoming a reality than anyone else's. He remains committed to the idea of some kind of lasting peace through negotiation, but regards the whole Palestinian problem as a political tightrope that he is reluctant to attempt to walk out on. He prefers to point to the progress he has made on the domestic front when talking about the achievements he has made in his reign of over thirty years. After years of war and unrest, Jordan is back on course in the growth and development plans begun in the 1960's and 1970's. There has been measurable success: unemployment is low, and the economy—based on agriculture, mining, and tourism—is growing at a respectable ten percent annually. More than half the population now lives in cities, including the Bedouins, who remain fiercely loyal to him. Domestic opposition has declined over the years. Early in his reign, Hussein had favored making Jordan a democracy, but over the years he changed his mind and now insists that his absolute monarchy is better for a country with such a diverse population.

His personal life brings him great happiness. In 1978, a year after the death of Princess Alia, he met Lisa Halaby. The daughter of an American businessman in the Middle East, Lisa knew Arabic and the customs of Jordan. Though some fifteen years younger than the king, she possessed a maturity beyond her years—similar to that of the king himself when he took the reins of power at a very young age. They were married in 1980 and have three children, bringing to a total of ten the number of children the king has. Hussein spends as much time as his busy schedule will allow enjoying his family and Queen Noor, as he renamed his bride. "Noor," in Arabic, means "light."

8

AYATOLLAH

RUHOLLAH

KHOMEINI

Iran

Ayatollah Ruhollah Khomeini

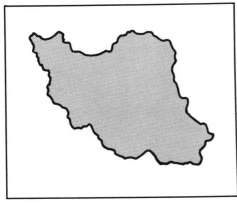

Iran

8

Ayatollah Ruhollah Khomeini is the only Middle Eastern leader who is a member of the Islamic clergy. A Shiite Moslem, he believes that the Islamic countries have come under too much influence from outside—especially Western—cultures. The revolution that he started in Iran in 1979 aims at ridding that country of this foreign influence and reviving the conservative Islamic customs and laws. Since 1982 Khomeini has hardly appeared in public at all. Outside observers speculate that the ayatollah, who is in his mid-eighties, has been weakened by age and a kidney disorder. It is difficult for outsiders to learn the truth because Iran is essentially closed to members of the world press. Whether or not he appears in public, the ayatollah remains powerful and is a major symbol of religious fundamentalism in the Middle East.

Ruhollah Mussavi Khomeini was born on May 17 in the early years of this century. (Some sources give the year as 1900, others say 1901 or 1902.) He was born in the small town of Khomein about 180 miles south of Teheran, the capital city of Iran. At that time Iran was called Persia and was under British influence.

Khomeini was the youngest of six children born to Sayed Mustafa Mussavi and his wife, Hajar Saghafi. When he was five months old his father, the head of the community, was killed while making a religious pilgrimage to Iraq. It is unclear whether the men who killed him were bandits, members of an enemy religious faction, or government officials sent by the ruling Qajar dynasty, but Khomeini's mother testified against her husband's murderers and they were executed. Khomeini and his brothers and sisters were reared by their mother and an aunt, who instilled in them a deep religious fervor and a strong sense of the importance of combatting all enemies of Islam. These included the British and members of other Moslem sects, whose beliefs, Khomeini's family was certain, would destroy the faith. As Shiite Moslems, the family belonged to the dominant sect in Persia.

By the time he was fifteen, Khomeini's mother and aunt had died, but his oldest brother continued to instill in him the family traditions and religious beliefs, and he showed real promise in religious studies. When he was nineteen, he moved to the city of Arak to study under the Ayatollah Abdul Karim Haeri, one of the foremost Islamic theologians of the day. When his instructor moved to Qum in 1922, Khomeini went with him. Qum had been a center for Shiite Moslems since early Islamic times. Haeri founded an institution of Islamic learning called the Madraseh Faizieh there, where Khomeini lived and taught for many years.

Khomeini studied not only Islamic law and Islamic mysticism but also the works of the Greek philosophers Aristotle and Plato. He would later use their writings as a basis for his model for an Islamic republic. He wrote poetry and taught philosophy, and at the age of twenty-eight he made the pilgrimage to Mecca that is obligatory for all Moslems. In the course of many years of studying and teaching, Khomeini gained a reputation as an alim, a religious scholar. He published twenty-one books and trained some twelve hundred men who make up the religious elite of his country. He was venerated by his students for his strict self-discipline and intense spiritual study. By the 1950's, when he was himself in his fifties, he had gathered enough followers to be recognized as one of several hundred Shiite leaders in his country honored with the title "ayatollah," which means "sign of God." By early 1960 his following was so great that he was known as Ayatollah al Ozma, or "grand ayatollah"— the highest religious title one can have, other than the Imam, and accorded to only five others.

In Shiite belief, all modern Moslem rulers are merely pretenders to their thrones; the last rightful ruler of Islam was Ali, the son-in-law of the Prophet Mohammed. One day, Shiites believe, Allah will send an Imam who will be not only the religious but also the political ruler of all Islam. In this belief, Shiites differ from Sunnis, who see a separation between religion and politics. Ayatollah Ruhollah Khomeini has always believed firmly in the Shiite doctrine.

During the years Khomeini was at Qum, studying and teaching at the Madraseh Faizieh, many changes took place in his country. The most important was its development as an independent nation free of control by either Russia or the British, who as recently as 1907 had agreed to divide Persia into various "spheres of influence." Not until 1921 did Russia withdraw all its occupying forces. That same year Riza Khan, an army officer, overthrew the Qajar dynasty, which had ruled since 1794. He established a military dictatorship and in 1925 was elected hereditary shah, founding the new Pahlavi dynasty.

It was under Riza Shah Pahlavi, in 1935, that Persia's name was changed to Iran. The shah introduced many reforms, encouraged the development of industry, and promoted education. Some religious leaders, among them Khomeini, charged that he was destroying Islamic culture. In response Pahlavi took steps to silence the criticism of the clergy.

During World War II Iran was occupied by British and Soviet forces. Riza Shah Pahlavi was felt by the British to be sympathetic to the Nazis, and in 1941 he was forced to abdicate in favor of his son, Mohammed Riza Pahlavi. In the mind of Khomeini, the new shah was even worse than his father because he was merely a puppet of the British and the Americans. When the United Nations voted to partition Palestine, Khomeini condemned what he called the "Washington-Tel Aviv-Teheran Axis," and when the shah visited Qum in 1953, Khomeini refused to stand in the traditional gesture of respect. He became one of the shah's most outspoken critics, always insisting that he was acting as a defender of Islam. Although the shah considered him a serious internal enemy, he did not let Khomeini's criticisms deter him from what he believed was the proper course for Iran.

The shah believed that Iran must be brought into the modern world; in his opinion, that meant adopting western customs. He initiated a broad program of economic and social changes, and inspired the wrath of even the most moderate clergymen. At the core of the problem were the agrarian and land reforms that deprived Shiite clergy of much of their property. Women's rights were another sore issue where the clergy were concerned. The real problem was that the shah's reform programs, in Khomeini's words, represented the "erosion of the clergy's dominance in matters of marriage, education and morals, and the destruction of the constitutional checks and balances that kept the legislation in harmony with Islamic law."

The shah overreacted to the clergy's resistance against his modernization plans: he sent forces against the Madraseh Faizieh in Qum, and some twenty young students were killed. Students in Teheran then staged a revolt against the shah. In the weeks that followed, the shah's forces killed many rioters and imposed martial law in the city. Resistance continued, however, and in 1963 the shah appealed to Khomeini to stop his relentless opposition. Khomeini refused and was put under house arrest for a year. That meant that he could not speak in public, and the shah hoped that the unrest would die down. It did not work out that way; Khomeini became a kind of martyr, and his cause grew in popularity.

In 1964, not long after he had been released from house arrest, Khomeini denounced an agreement that the government had made with the United States under which American military forces were exempted from prosecution in Iranian courts. The ayatollah called the agreement "undue submission to foreign domination." He resented the fact that the shah was receiving American military aid in return for Iranian oil. This latest agreement seemed to him just one more example of the shah's submission to the United States.

At last the shah sent Khomeini into exile. He went first to Turkey. But there Iranian students waged large demonstrations on his behalf, and the Turkish authorities also sent him away. Next he went to Iraq, settling, in 1965, in Najaf in the southern part of the country, near the tomb of Ali, the son-in-law of the Prophet Mohammed.

In exile the ayatollah headed a theological school. In his lectures, he continued to voice his opposition to the shah and called for political action to weed out foreign corruption and Western influences, which he firmly believed were contrary to Islamic law. By this time, he was calling for the overthrow of the shah's regime and its replacement by an Islamic republic. Khomeini kept in touch with his followers and reinforced their belief in his principles by sending taped messages secretly into Iran—perhaps through the good offices of followers who came as pilgrims to visit Islamic holy places in Iraq. His supporters listened to them in mosques all over the country. Hearing of the messages, the shah's secret police started a campaign against Khomeini supporters, but this campaign only increased Khomeini's ranks inside Iran.

During the late 1960's and early 1970's, the need for oil on the part of the Western industrial countries gave rise to an economic boom in Iran. The country experienced unprecedented economic growth, and for a time the majority of Iranians had no quarrel with the shah, for they enjoyed a high standard of living. In times of prosperity, there is usually little social unrest. The shah was at the peak of his power, and Khomeini's influence was temporarily overshadowed. Still Khomeini persevered, holding fast to his beliefs and continuing to teach hard-line Islamic doctrine. He won the recognition and support of Yasir Arafat—the leader of the Palestinian Liberation Organization—who visited him in Iraq in the early 1970's. When the shah held an elaborate celebration honoring his dynasty, the ayatollah, from Iraq, denounced the feast as extravagant.

As the 1970's wore on, the Iranian people began to grow discontented again. Most ordinary Iranians had not benefited as much as they had hoped from the economic boom. Moreover, they were neither politically nor socially ready. The religious leaders had remained independent of the shah's new-image policy, and thus it became the logical vehicle for revolutionary—which in this case meant conservative—sentiments. Khomeini, though still in exile, was the natural leader of this movement.

Khomeini and other religious leaders increased their criticism of the shah and organized protests. The shah responded to this new unrest with oppressive measures. In 1977 the ayatollah's son Mustafa was killed under mysterious circumstances; Khomeini believed that the killing had been done on the shah's direct orders. Now Khomeini took direct action. He sent an open letter to the Iranians, calling for the armed forces to deliver the country to the people. Mass demonstrations followed, and the demonstrators carried flags and banners emblazoned with the face of the ayatollah. The shah fought back by persuading the Iraqi government to expel Khomeini, who then took up residence in France and added Saddam Hussein, president of Iraq, to his list of enemies.

Having established a new headquarters in a small town outside Paris, Khomeini used the international press to pursue his cause. He used the telephone to make contacts in Teheran, calling for strikes and demonstrations that were carried out by his supporters at home. Young men like Sadegh Ghotbzadeh worked tirelessly to keep the revolutionary fires burning until Khomeini could return to Iran.

By the late 1970's, the shah was losing control of his people. On December 28, 1978, he designated Dr. Shahpur Bakhtiar, a leader of the National Front, to form a new civilian government to take power on January 6, 1979. It was a desperation move that came too late. The shah left Iran on January 16, saying he was going on vacation, and Bakhtiar assumed power with a nine-member regency council.

It was obvious to everyone that the shah had no intention of returning to Iran, and Khomeini immediately announced his intention to return. On February 1, 1979, he rode triumphantly through the streets of Teheran, amid the cheers and shouts of millions of admiring followers.

Khomeini quickly took advantage of his power. He threatened to have Bakhtiar and his aides arrested if they refused to step aside, and the Bakhtiar government resigned. Khomeini then set up a Council of the Islamic Republic of Iran, which named Mehdi Bazargan as prime minister. Then he returned to Qum, where he established his headquarters on March 1. From Teheran a new constitution was drafted that gave Khomeini supreme power over public and military affairs. Bazargan's government in Teheran was merely a front.

One of the first things Khomeini did was to sever relations with Israel and to recognize the PLO. As a staunch defender of Islam, he did not acknowledge the legitimacy of Israel. Yet he promised the 30,000 Jews living in Iran that their rights would be safeguarded. Then he attended to Iran's internal affairs. He set up tribunals that sentenced six hundred or more of the shah's officials to death, among them the former prime minister, Amir Abbas Hoveida. The shah himself was condemned in absentia, and Khomeini promised that the shah would never be allowed to return to Iran.

Next, Khomeini ordered a purge of all "undesirables" in Iran, defining as undesirable homosexuals, prostitutes, adulterers, and those who had insulted the Imam (himself). He reinstituted rigid Islamic codes, and suddenly Iranians were subjected to a drastic shift in lifestyle. Women were forced to wear the traditional head coverings. Alcoholic beverages, coeducation, mixed swimming, and movies were prohibited. So was Western music, which the ayatollah said "stupefied persons listening and made their brains inactive and frivolous." By the end of the summer of 1979, Western journalists had been expelled from the country, the offices of many magazines and newspapers had been closed, and those that were still publishing were subject to extreme censorship—any newspaper that was printed had to print only the truth, as Khomeini saw it.

Many Iranians resented these restrictions. They had hated the shah because he had taken much of the country's oil wealth for himself and because he had tried to put down the unrest in Iran with repressive measures. They had believed the charges of Khomeini and other religious leaders that the shah cared nothing for Iranian and Islamic traditions. They had not expected to be forced to go back to nineteenth-century ways. Some of Khomeini's closest aides were assassinated, and he retaliated with a harsh crackdown that equalled the shah's reign of terror. In September 1979, the government troops, acting on the ayatollah's direct orders, brutally suppressed an uprising by the Kurds, a fiercely independent group who live in northwestern Iran.

Amid all this upheaval, the day-to-day workings of the government suffered greatly. Inflation was rampant, oil production was practically at a standstill, foreign trade and investment abruptly ended, and some three million people were out of work. Most of the people who had been trained as managers fled the country, and there was no experienced civil service staff to keep the country running. Countries that depended on Iranian oil were dismayed by Khomeini's actions. Even the Soviet Union called him a religious fanatic. The United States was worried about its oil supplies from Iran, but American officials were cautious about speaking against Khomeini. They tried to negotiate with the Khomeini government to ensure the continuation of trade.

Unfortunately, United States officials were not as cautious as they should have been in their dealings with the shah. By the fall of 1979 representatives of the shah were trying to get the United States to grant him asylum. The shah had been staunchly anti-Communist and had been a major Middle Eastern ally of the United States, granting the United States favorable oil trade arrangements and allowing American oil companies to operate in Iran. What seems to have persuaded President Jimmy Carter to allow the shah to come to the United States at this time, however, was the news that the exiled ruler was gravely ill with a blood disease, a form of cancer. He could get the best medical treatment in the world in the United States, and Carter could not bring himself to deny the shah that treatment. The problem was that Carter and his advisers failed to understand the extent of Khomeini's power and to anticipate how fiercely Khomeini would react to their granting asylum to the ayatollah's most hated enemy.

On November 3, 1979, militant followers of Khomeini seized the American embassy in Teheran. They stoned the embassy, burned the American flag, trampled pictures of President Carter, and took ninety hostages, sixty-two of them Americans.

Having long regarded the United States as the source of many of Iran's troubles and one of the greatest enemies of Islam, the ayatollah took great pleasure in keeping the hostages. And despite intense efforts to negotiate their release, plus a risky attempt to rescue them that failed, the United States was not able to secure the return of the hostages until January 20, 1981, after 444 days of captivity. During this time, the shah had left the United States and after spending time in Panama, had gone at last to Egypt, where President Anwar el-Sadat had offered his old friend asylum. The shah died of cancer there a few months later, on July 27, 1980.

The seizing of the United States embassy in Teheran seemed to signal a new stage in the fundamentalist Islamic revolution that Khomeini had begun. A little more than two weeks later, armed religious zealots, influenced by Khomeini, seized the Grand Mosque in Mecca. Although Saudi Arabian forces were able to recapture the mosque, the Saudis and other Arab countries feared that Khomeini intended to export his revolution. No one was more concerned about this threat than President Saddam Hussein of Iraq. Iraq shares its longest (western) border with Iran, and Hussein already knew that he was high on the ayatollah's list of personal enemies.

In 1978, when Khomeini was still in exile in France, a reporter had asked him who his enemies were. "First the shah," Khomeini had answered, "then the American Satan, then Saddam Hussein and his infidel Baath Party." It was obvious to Saddam Hussein, in late 1979, that he was the only one on the list who had not yet felt the force of Khomeini's hatred.

Their personal enmity went back to the time when Khomeini was in exile in Iraq's holy city of Najaf. He had been arrested several times there for anti-shah activities, and in 1975, Hussein had ordered him placed under house arrest. Three years later, when the shah was being increasingly pressured by Islamic fundamentalists operating with Khomeini's backing, Hussein, who was fearful of the Shiite population in his own country, had agreed to expel Khomeini. Added to his purely personal reason for hating the Iraqi president was Khomeini's hatred of Hussein's philosophy of government. Iraq's is a socialist regime and one that strictly separates church and state, while Khomeini has always insisted on the clergy's God-given right to rule an Islamic country.

In Khomeini's plan for the Middle East, Iraq was a natural "sister Islamic republic." Not only did the two countries share a common border, but Shiite Moslems make up a fifty-five percent majority of Iraq's population; and two of the most important Shiite shrines are in Iraq, in Najaf and Karbala. Although Saddam Hussein was a popular leader who had modernized Iraq without alienating the various religious cults that oppose western influence, he was himself a Sunni Moslem, and he was aware that a strong appeal to the religious fervor of the Shiite majority might spell trouble for him. Thus, Hussein was very concerned about containing the "aggressive and expansionist" Islamic revolution that had started in Iran.

In September 1980, in the middle of the American hostage crisis, Iraqi forces invaded Iran, blowing up some of its most productive oil fields and capturing Iranian border lands. Despite its internal economic and political problems, Iran quickly mobilized to resist the Iraqi invasion. A curious assortment of professional soldiers, religious mullahs, neighborhood militiamen, and schoolboys managed to stave off the Iraqi assault and continue to fight back against the invaders. What seems to hold them together is their religious fervor. One youth told a *New York Times* reporter that he was proud to be on the front because he was fighting for the cause of Islam. He was a member of the Besage, or Mobilization, one of the newest Iranian revolutionary groups formed by the ayatollah. Led into battle with the cry "God is great!" these young Iranians are willing to die for Islam.

The war that began with the Iraqi invasion of Iran has, with the exception of the constant war between the Arabs and Israel, lasted longer than any other conflict between two Middle East countries. By May 1982, Iran's ragtag forces, under a plan called Operation Jerusalem, had recaptured 2,116 square miles of Iranian territory, including 106 miles of land along the border. In June 1982, Saddam Hussein declared a cease-fire, withdrew his troops, and asked for peace. The ayatollah would have none of that; he called for the resignation of Hussein and the overthrow of the ruling Baath Party.

The war has created strange political alliances. Israeli Prime Minister Menachem Begin supported Iran in order to cause trouble for Saddam Hussein, whom Israel has long regarded as its primary enemy in the Arab world. Thus America's ally contributed to the ayatollah's war machine. Saddam Hussein also relies on Egyptian military aid and reestablished diplomatic ties with Egypt, after breaking them over the Camp David accords. No Arab leader denounced Anwar el-Sadat more harshly than did Saddam Hussein, but to pursue his war against Iran he has been willing to accept help from Sadat's successor, Hosni Mubarak.

In early June 1982, the Soviet Union urged Iran to make peace with Iraq and proposed that the two countries would do better to unite with it in establishing an anti-imperialist front in the Middle East. Khomeini refused to agree saying: "The Americans fear that the Soviet Union might do this or that in the region if we defeat Iraq. The Soviet Union can do nothing. It has proved to be capable of nothing."

President Assad of Syria is perhaps Iran's strongest supporter, and the PLO is furious with Khomeini for refusing to end the war. The PLO also does not like Khomeini's plan to capture Jerusalem one day, for the PLO dreams of Jerusalem as the capital of an independent Palestinian state. There is an old saying that "politics makes strange bedfellows," and nowhere has this been more true than in the Middle East.

During this time, while Khomeini continued to wage his revolution outside the borders of Iran, he was by no means securely in power in his own country; internal strife seemed never ending. Eventually several of the nonreligious leaders who had supported the ayatollah's revolution were executed or exiled. One of the best-known victims of the revolution was Sadegh Ghotbzadeh, Iran's foreign minister. As spokesman for the Teheran government during the hostage crisis, his face became familiar to millions of television viewers throughout the world. He had been with Khomeini for several years and had been the ayatollah's interpreter and political adviser in Paris. He was charged with plotting to assassinate Khomeini. Although he denied the charge, he had, indeed, lost faith in the man whom he had long supported. In September 1982, on orders from Khomeini, he was shot. In a letter smuggled out by friends, the condemned man wrote: "I saw the light and tried as best I could to undo the damage I had done in terms of supporting the satanic regime of the mullahs." President Abolhassan Bani-Sadr also fell into disfavor; he managed to escape to Paris.

The most organized opposition to the ayatollah has come from a group called the Mujahedeen Khalq. It was founded in 1965 and was helpful in overthrowing the shah, but after the revolution of 1979, the group split over the clergy-dominated regime of Khomeini. The anti-Khomeini faction now works to overthrow his government. Since 1981 it has been responsible for a number of bloody insurrections and for the assassination of President Mohammed Ali Rajai and other government figures. It is believed that the Mujahedeen were responsible for the explosion that destroyed the suburban Paris house where Khomeini had lived while in exile in France. The morning after the bombing, French police found a crude figure that was supposed to represent the ayatollah hanging from a tree in the garden.

Some of Khomeini's own supporters have been responsible for much of Iran's internal strife. The mullahs have proved overzealous in their efforts to purge Iran of secular and western influences. Once they had eliminated their secular opponents, they turned on each other, and Khomeini was forced to issue a warning against factionalism within the ranks of his Islamic Republican party. According to some observers, the only thing the mullahs agreed on was that women should wear the traditional chador, an item of clothing that totally covers the body except for the eyes. They even ordered all women to have new photographs taken for their identification cards that show them with their heads covered and their faces only partially visible.

The mullahs disagreed on so many things that they left the average Iranian in a state of fear and confusion. The various revolutionary guards and committees that made up the ruling structure acted quite independently of each other. Until recently, they had the power to tap telephones, spy on the conduct of

Iranians in their own homes, and investigate the backgrounds of all Iranians who came to their attention. To add to the confusion, they often overlapped in authority. Thus, an Iranian citizen might be considered innocent by the standards of one committee, but that did not mean he could breathe a sigh of relief. The next day another committee could decide that he was, indeed, guilty of some crime against Islam. For a while, the ayatollah himself contributed to this state of confusion. He decreed that all government workers must take a test to see how well they knew Islamic law. He urged schoolchildren to spy on their teachers, neighbors on neighbors.

Amid the turmoil, many educated Iranians left the country, often crossing the border, at great risk, into Turkey or Pakistan. Their flight, coupled with the effects of the war with Iraq, was devastating. The Iranian economy was in a shambles. Food shortages were common, and items such as soap, china, drinking glasses, kitchen utensils, cameras, film, washers, dryers, and automobile parts were in short supply. Industry did not recover, and business confidence was low. Ordinary Iranians were so insecure about what was acceptable behavior that they lost any sense of being able to control their own destinies. This led to low morale and a drop in levels of productivity on the part of those workers who did have jobs—and many did not. The internal situation was critical, and moderate voices in the Islamic Republican Party appealed to Khomeini to do something to stabilize the country and to present a less threatening image to the rest of the world. The prevailing world opinion was that Khomeini was a fanatic, and as long as that image remained, Iran could not expect much help in its efforts to bring about an economic recovery.

At last, in December 1982, Khomeini moved to curb the excesses and brutalities of the revolutionary guards and committees. In an eight-point proclamation, he forbade the revolutionary bodies to invade the privacy of Iranian citizens, urged the courts to observe the traditions of Islamic justice, offered a limited pardon to those who had been prosecuted by excessive means, and called for the formation of committees to look into the activities of the revolutionary courts and to hear citizens' complaints. Many observers were skeptical about the plan, pointing out that it was a risky policy for the ayatollah to adopt.

According to Shaul Bakhash, an expert on the Middle East at Princeton University, the ayatollah's proclamation aimed at curbing the powers of the very organizations on which he had relied for support. Also, it seemed to reverse his own policies about the violation of privacy—how could he have urged schoolchildren to spy on their teachers and then say that such spying was a crime.? Might not the new committees formed to hear citizens' complaints find evidence that some of Khomeini's closest supporters had been guilty of excesses? In the end, his new policies may simply add to the confusion and threaten to undermine his regime even further.

It will take time to learn the answers to these questions. And only time will tell if Khomeini's Islamic revolution will succeed in Iran, and in the rest of the Moslem world. Time is one thing the ayatollah does not have much more of. Aging, gaunt, and in poor health, he cannot seriously believe that Allah will keep him alive long enough to see the successful conclusion of his revolution. There has been talk of a successor. Elections were held to select an Assembly of Experts to choose the man to succeed him. But there is such political apathy in Iran—such a feeling of "what's the use?"—that turnout for the elections was embarrassingly low. For now, the ayatollah's is the voice of authority in Iran, but there is some question about how strong it will continue to be, or how long it will continue to be heard.

9

HOSNI
~~~~~~~~~~~~~~~~~~~~~~~~~~

MUBARAK
~~~~~~~~~~~~~~~~~~~~~~~~~~

Egypt

Hosni Mubarak

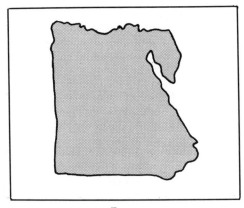

Egypt

9

"I swear by God almighty to faithfully safeguard the republican system, to honor the constitution and law, to protect fully the people's interests and to safeguard the country's independence and the safety of its territories."

This is the constitutional oath that Mohamed Hosni Mubarak took at the special joint session of the People's Assembly and the Shura Council in Cairo, Egypt, on October 14, 1981. The events of the previous eight days had been nightmarish. Anwar el-Sadat, president of Egypt, had been assassinated while reviewing, with Vice President Mubarak, a parade commemorating the 1973 October War. Mubarak himself had been wounded. Four accused killers and twenty accomplices had been arrested. Now Mubarak was formally succeeding to the presidency.

Still wearing bandages, the new president delivered his inaugural address, a tribute to his "commander, leader, father and brother—Mohammed Anwar el-Sadat."

"The whole civilized world has been shocked by this loss," said Mubarak. "Its feelings have been shaken by the tragedy of the loss of the proud leader. This leader opened for the millions, for all the people, new and broad vistas of hope for a peace encompassing the whole of mankind. He opened these vistas through his stunning decisions, his legendary and extraordinary courage, his deep and sound wisdom and his strong and gigantic will with which he braved the most dangerous storms and horrors."

Mubarak promised his people—and the world—peace, security, and stability, and he vowed to remain loyal to the Camp David agreements and Egypt's peace treaty with Israel. He ended his speech with these words: "We will proceed on our great road, not stopping and not hesitating, building and not destroying, protecting and not threatening, preserving and not wasting." It was the type of speech that Anwar el-Sadat might have made; but there the similarities between the new president and the late president ended.

Sadat had been a unique personality—a risk-taker, a man of extraordinary vision and courage. He was one of the most famous leaders in the world. Mubarak was a quiet man who had never been in the world spotlight; in fact, he was a virtual unknown. Filling the shoes of Sadat was going to be a tough job for Hosni Mubarak.

Mohamed Hosni Mubarak was born on May 4, 1928, in the Nile Delta village of Kafr el-Meselha in the province of Minufiya. (Ten years earlier, Anwar el-Sadat had been born in the same province.) One of five children of an inspector of the Egyptian Ministry of Justice, Mubarak attended local schools and after graduation from high school entered the national military academy. He graduated in February 1949, commissioned as a lieutenant, and then spent a year at the air force academy, training as a pilot. By 1952 he was training other Egyptian pilots.

In that year, King Farouk of Egypt was toppled in a coup led by General Gamal Abdel Nasser. The coup marked the end of the Egyptian monarchy that had held power since 1922, when Great Britain granted Egypt its independence. Nasser vowed to set up a more representative form of government and to rid Egypt of foreign domination, for he believed that under the monarchy, Egypt had been a mere puppet of the West.

In 1956 Nasser—who ran unopposed—was elected president of Egypt and began to institute a more socialistic kind of government. He called for land reform and for economic and social development that would benefit all the people of Egypt, not just the privileged. While determined to be independent of Western domination, he was willing to work with the West in ways that helped Egypt, just as he was willing to work with the Soviet Union, which had offered him military equipment and training for his forces. A major aspect of his plans for the economic development of his country was the building of a dam at Aswan, which was to provide electrical power and to help irrigate some of the arid lands. Nasser asked the Western countries and the Soviet Union for help in its construction. When Great Britain and France refused this aid, Nasser nationalized the Suez Canal.

Built in the 1860's by the investor-owned Suez Canal Company, the canal connected the Mediterranean Sea with the Gulf of Suez and was a major shipping artery in the Middle East. European forces quickly stepped in to retake it, and Israel, denied use of the canal by Egypt since its founding in 1948, joined them, causing Nasser and the Egyptians to become even more bitter toward Israel. Nasser continued to refuse Israel the right to use it. He also turned increasingly to the Soviet Union for aid in pursuing his policies for his country.

The Soviet Union was particularly generous with military equipment and training for the Egyptians, and between 1952 and 1959 Hosni Mubarak traveled there twice for further pilot training. On his return, he shared with his own pilot trainees the things he had learned. As a trainer of pilots, Mubarak gained an excellent reputation for fairness. Although his students included several of his own cousins and a brother of Anwar el-Sadat—at that time a top aide of Nasser's who had been with the president since before the coup that brought him to power—Mubarak showed no partiality to these young men. Mubarak was also respected for his skills as a pilot and an organizer, and by 1967 he had been named commander of the Egyptian air force academy.

In that year Nasser, a sworn foe of Israel, blockaded the Israeli port of Elat and obtained the withdrawal of the United Nations forces on the Sinai Peninsula, who were there to keep peace between Egypt and Israel. These and other provocations caused Israel to launch a full-scale attack on its Arab neighbors.

Not only did Israel capture areas belonging to Syria, Jordan, and Egypt, but its attack devastated the military forces of these countries. All Egyptians felt humiliated by the defeat. Mubarak was given the assignment of reconstructing the Egyptian Air Force into one that would be capable not only of resisting future attacks but of launching successful invasions. He fulfilled his assignment and in 1969 was promoted to Commander in Chief of the Air Force and also became deputy minister of war.

Also in 1967, Anwar el-Sadat became vice-president of Egypt under Nasser, and in 1970, on Nasser's death from a heart attack, Sadat became president.

One of the first things Sadat did as president was to break relations with the Soviet Union and expel the seventeen thousand Russian military advisers who were in Egypt. He had long believed that Nasser was too close to the Russians and that the Soviet Union wanted to control Egyptian policy through their military supplies and advisers. He felt that Nasser's relationship with the Russians had been too much like King Farouk's relationship with the West. He wanted Egypt to be free of any kind of foreign domination.

Having thus established Egypt's independence, Sadat concentrated on his other goals for his country. He wanted to modernize it and raise its people's standard of living. He wanted to make trade agreements that would benefit Egypt with any country that was willing. Most of all, he wanted to reestablish Egypt as a country worthy of respect in the eyes of the rest of the world. Egypt's position in the world, and its own self-respect, had been severely damaged in 1967 when it had been embarrassingly defeated by Israel. That Israel had also seized Egyptian lands then added to Egypt's shame.

Accordingly, Sadat ordered Egyptian military forces to prepare for a strike against Israel, and in October 1973, Egypt attacked Israeli fortifications in the Sinai peninsula. General Mubarak engineered and led the successful air strike that paved the way for the Suez Canal crossing that enabled Egyptian troops to breach the Israeli lines. For his heroic role, he was promoted to the rank of major general.

This time Egypt's forces fought well, and Sadat believed that he had succeeded in showing the rest of the world that his country's fighting ability should not be underrated. Although Israel had been caught unawares by the Egyptian attack—which came on the most solemn of Jewish holidays—it quickly marshalled its forces, and aided by the United States, it moved to retain control of the territories it had held since 1967. Other Arab countries, impressed by Egypt's fine military showing, backed Egypt in the war and withheld their oil from the United States. But Sadat's forces were under severe Israeli pressure, and he agreed to a cease-fire and negotiations that would return to Egypt the lands that Israel had seized six years before.

The United States acted as the chief negotiator between the two sides in the peace talks. Secretary of State Henry Kissinger shuttled back and forth between Cairo and Jerusalem, trying to find a way to bring the warring sides together. One of the results of the negotiations was that Sadat agreed to reopen the Suez Canal, which had been closed since the June 1967 war. Israeli shipping and trade had always suffered as a result of their not being able to use the canal. Its complete shutdown caused the shipping industries of many other countries to suffer, too. During this time, Egypt also had to sacrifice; it lost the large yearly revenues it had previously earned from fees for the use of the waterway. Other Arab countries helped out by subsidizing the Egyptian economy with contributions roughly equalling the annual revenues from the canal. Sadat now believed that Egypt would be better off financially if it reopened the canal and resumed collecting its fees than if it continued to rely on its Arab neighbors for help. He also realized that opening the canal would be a gesture of peace. The Suez Canal was reopened on June 5, 1975.

Less than two months earlier, on April 15, 1975, Sadat had named Mohamed Hosni Mubarak as his vice-president. This meant that he had chosen Mubarak as his political heir, and the appointment came as a surprise to many Egyptians, as well as to most of the outside world. Mubarak was not at all well-known; but Sadat had had his eye on him since the early 1950's, when Sadat was a member of Nasser's inner circle and Mubarak was a young bomber pilot. Something about Mubarak had impressed Sadat enough to cause him to write the young pilot's name in his notebook. It was Sadat who had appointed him to head the

Egyptian Air Force and to be deputy minister of war. Sadat had taken to calling Egyptians who were capable of dealing with the Israelis and the rest of the world from a position of strength "October men," referring to the fine Egyptian showing in the 1973 October War; he considered Mubarak the epitome of an "October man."

As vice-president, Mubarak took on the role of improving Egypt's relations with other countries. He visited European capitals to discuss diplomatic and trade relations. He visited Africa and established closer ties with some of the newly independent African nations. He made trips to other Arab capitals and developed close ties to Arab leaders and politicians. In 1979 he visited China, met with Chairman Mao Tse-Tung, and negotiated agreements under which China would supply arms to Egypt. He kept a very low profile through all this, and many people considered him a mere shadow of Sadat. A lot of ordinary Egyptians knew him only from photographs of meetings with Sadat, and some referred to him as the "man who goes to meetings."

The diplomatic negotiations in the spotlight during the late 1970's were those between Sadat and Menachem Begin, prime minister of Israel. Sadat had made the unprecedented move—for an Arab leader—of visiting Jerusalem, speaking at the Israeli Knesset, and praying at the al-Aqsa Mosque there. He had agreed that Israel had a right to exist.

Like most other Arabs, Sadat had regarded Israel as his enemy all his life, and it had been very difficult for him to change his mind. But there were practical reasons why he had decided to negotiate. He had put so many of his country's resources into fighting Israel that his people were suffering: There were riots in Cairo and Alexandria because there was not enough food. He wanted a chance to channel some of Egypt's resources into internal programs. Sadat also had moral reasons for thinking about changing his attitude toward Israel. He had lost a brother in the Six-Day War and had come to believe that all the bloodshed was wrong. He may also have been influenced by President Carter. Carter had written letters to Sadat asking him to consider making peace with Israel. He wrote in a letter back to Carter: "He who cannot change the very fabric of his thought will never be able to change reality, and will never, therefore, make any progress."

With the United States acting as a liaison, Sadat and Begin began to talk about peace. What came out of their negotiations was the historic peace treaty signed in March 1979. While the treaty did not address the Palestinian question, it was a major step toward peace in the Middle East. In December 1978 Sadat and Begin shared the Nobel Peace Prize for their efforts.

Sadat became a hero in the West and in Israel. He was not so well thought of in the rest of the Arab world or even in his own country. Other Arabs had not had the same change of heart that he had. Eighteen Arab countries labeled him a traitor and imposed economic and political sanctions against Egypt. Even Saudi Arabia, regarded by Sadat as Egypt's greatest ally, refused to support him. Nor had many of his own people changed their ideas about Israel. Over ninety percent of Egyptians are Sunni Moslems. Although they vary in their ideas about how strictly they should keep the faith, the majority of them hate Israel. Some of Sadat's own countrymen began to plot against him.

Sadat would not allow these criticisms to dissuade him. He pushed on, engaging in the Palestinian autonomy talks provided for under the Camp David accords, even though major spokesmen for the Palestinians refused to take part in them. And then, he offered asylum to the Shah of Iran.

By sheltering his old friend, Sadat exposed himself to considerable danger. The revolution against the shah in Iran had been led by Shiite Moslem followers of the Ayatollah Khomeini. There were Shiites in Egypt, and Sadat was aware that they might try to assassinate him if he let the shah into Egypt. Sadat could not forget, though, that the shah had supplied Egypt with the oil it had desperately needed to wage the October 1973 war. Now that the shah was very ill, Sadat could not in good conscience deny him a haven. He may have paid for this compassion with his life.

The men who assassinated Sadat on October 6, 1981, were members of a group of religious fundamentalists. They hated him for harboring the shah and for signing a treaty with Israel. They hated him as well because they believed he was westernizing Egypt and turning his back on the old Islamic values. They might have killed him for any one of these so-called crimes.

The assassination of Sadat was not unexpected, even by Sadat himself, for Moslem fanatics hated him. Nevertheless, it saddened the world. Even his bitterest enemies had to admit that he was a unique man—unique in his vision, strong in his character, charismatic in his personality. He was a true statesman, and whether one agreed with him or not, he had impressed himself on the hearts and minds of the non-Arab world in a way that no other Arab had done in a very long time.

When Hosni Mubarak took over as Sadat's successor, he knew very well that comparisons between himself and his predecessor would be made for a long time to come. Mubarak had a different approach, a different style. Sadat had enjoyed luxurious surroundings; Mubarak liked simple ones. His office in Cairo's Ouruba Palace was spartan compared to Sadat's. Sadat's schedule was unpredictable; often he would work a few hours and then leave for a long walk in the country. Mubarak, on the other hand, worked long hours, usually beginning at dawn. Sadat liked to make public appearances and could win over many audiences by the sheer force of his personality; Mubarak preferred to work quietly and to make few public appearances. He guarded his privacy and kept his family out of the public eye; in fact, he did not allow photographs to be taken of his wife, Susanna. Sadat was a consummate politician; Mubarak knew that his strength was in managing, not politicking. Sadat was an innovator; Mubarak was an implementer.

Mubarak long ago recognized these differences. He did not intend to become a second Sadat. He did not feel that Sadat had wanted a carbon copy of himself, and he did not want to be a carbon copy of Sadat. When he took his oath of office, he pledged to carry on much of the work that Sadat had begun, but he also suggested that his approach would be different. Mubarak's supporters say that he is exactly what Egypt needs now—a strong administrator who can get the job done.

The immediate job was to restore internal peace. Mubarak moved quickly to stabilize the country and to squelch all rumors of a coup. Sadat's assassins—those who had actually fired shots as well as those who had been involved in the plot—were quickly brought to trial, and in April 1982 they were executed. Mubarak released political prisoners whom Sadat had imprisoned several months earlier. He appointed a new cabinet, placing in the economic posts men who he believed would help improve Egypt's financial condition.

Egypt is a country in transition. It has many problems, and its future will depend on how those problems are met. Mubarak feels that more attention must be paid to the conditions of life of the people of Egypt. Most of them still cannot read or write, and there is a huge gap between the very wealthy and the very poor. Unemployment is a serious problem, even for those who have college degrees. Government birth control programs have failed; more than half the Egyptian population is under the age of fifteen. Cairo, the most modern city in Egypt, has close to twelve million people jammed into an area designed to accommodate only one million. Other cities are even worse, containing some of the worst slums in the world, packed with the unemployed and the influx of farmers who have abandoned country life. The people's needs are many, and they are already impatient with the conditions under which they must live. Unfortunately, no Egyptian leader can make the situation better overnight.

Mubarak agrees with the view of many economists that Egypt's main economic problem is the lack of an industrial base. Industry requires investment, and investment capital inside the country is very limited. Egypt needs to attract foreign investors who are willing to put money into industries that will boost the sluggish economy. In order to attract foreign capital Mubarak has begun a campaign to try to persuade foreign businesses that Egypt is stable enough politically to allow them to invest there without undue concern about the safety of their investments. He has also offered concessions to foreign investors to try to make doing business in Egypt more attractive.

In addition, Mubarak knows that Egyptian stability depends on that of the Middle East and has been active on the regional and international diplomatic fronts—areas in which he has had a good deal of experience. Under Sadat, he made many trips abroad, and he was also Sadat's confidant, for Sadat believed that state secrets should be known by more than one person.

Since he has been in power, Mubarak has demonstrated a more evenhanded approach to foreign relations than his predecessor.

He has tried to establish better relations with other Arab countries. Sadat openly attacked Arab leaders for responding negatively to his peace efforts. Mubarak will not publicly criticize other Arabs and has forbidden the Egyptian press to do it. Not even Libya's Muammar el-Qaddafi, who had been Mubarak's most outspoken critic, is exempt. When Sadat signed the Camp David accords, Qaddafi closed the border between the two countries. Mubarak reestablished diplomatic relations with Libya, and on February 1, 1982, the Libyan government re-opened the border, allowing Egyptians working in Libya to return home for visits.

Other Arab leaders have responded to Mubarak's overtures. King Hassan of Morocco was the first Arab leader to visit Egypt since the Arab states had broken off relations with Cairo in 1978. King Hussein of Jordan sent a congratulatory message to the Egyptian president after Israel returned the Sinai Peninsula to Egypt—in accordance with the Israeli-Egyptian peace treaty of 1979. Iraq has accepted military help from Mubarak in its war against Iran, and the Saudi Arabian leaders have made favorable public statements about him. In July 1982 Mubarak was invited to attend a summit meeting of nonaligned nations in Iraq. It was yet another step toward the reconciliation of Egypt with the rest of the Arab world, and many observers feel that it is only a matter of time before Egypt will again be fully accepted by most of her Arab neighbors.

So far, Mubarak has been able to accomplish the normalization of relations with his Arab brethren while working to fulfill the peace treaty with Israel, as he promised he would. He has not, however, tried to establish the same warm ties that Sadat enjoyed. When Israeli troops attacked PLO bases in Lebanon in 1982, Mubarak spoke out against them. During a visit to the United States, he stated that the policy of the Israeli government in continuing to establish settlements on the occupied West Bank was a serious obstacle to peace. As he told a reporter for *The New York Times* in January 1983, "Efforts must be exerted to bring about a total freeze of settlement activities." Like

Sadat—and nearly every other Middle East leader—Mubarak feels that the peace and stability of the entire region depend more on the settlement of the Palestinian question than on any other issue, and he is willing to speak out against Israel, or any other country, that threatens to undermine progress toward Palestinian self-rule.

Mubarak has not yet held office long enough to make a lasting mark on either the foreign or the domestic policies of his country. It is doubtful that he will ever have the public relations impact of his predecessor, but his low-key, moderate style may prove in the end to be better for the Egyptian people and the people of the Middle East.

10

MUAMMAR
EL-QADDAFI

Libya

Muammar el-Qaddafi

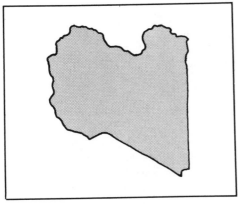
Libya

10

Libya, a country in northern Africa, has not always been considered part of the Middle East. Although it was part of the British Middle East Command during World War II, after the war it was more closely associated with the other countries of North Africa. It shares its eastern border with Egypt, is rich in oil resources, and is predominantly Moslem, but only after Muammar el-Qaddafi assumed power in 1969 did Libya again firmly establish a close relationship with the other countries of the Middle East. Qaddafi is a devout Moslem and a strong supporter of Arab nationalism. He is an implacable foe of Israel and has long given support to Palestinian guerrilla groups. By current definition, then, Libya is very much a part of the Middle East and Qaddafi, its "Brother Colonel," is one of the region's best-known leaders. Qaddafi has not forgotten Libya's place in North African politics either; indeed, he has tried very hard to influence the policies of that region, too. At times it is difficult to know just where Qaddafi's allegiance and real interests lie.

Muammar el-Qaddafi is a mysterious man. He guards his privacy jealously, and it is difficult to analyze the public man without knowledge of the private personality. Answering the question "Who is Qaddafi?" is like trying to put together a puzzle with several pieces missing. Something as seemingly simple as verifying the English spelling of his name is difficult. There are seven variations, and sometimes there are several different ones used in the same newspaper. Even pinpointing the exact place and date of his birth is difficult and leaves researchers in a dilemma. It is known that Muammar el-Qaddafi was born somewhere in the Libyan desert in 1942, but that is all that is known for sure.

Qaddafi's first influence was the desert. His family were Bedouins who earned a modest living raising livestock and growing barley near the town of Sidra. Desert living is hard, and people teach their children early to be tough in order to survive. Survival in the desert means a constant struggle against the extremes of heat and cold, drought, pestilence, and war. Except for war, all these enemies are in the nature of the desert, and desert people regard their home with awe and respect. Almost like a god, it is capable of giving and taking away, and mere men do not seem to have any control over their lives in it. Yet, there is something so permanent about the desert that its people generally prefer it to more civilized areas.

Qaddafi feels that way. He returns to the desert in times of personal crisis or when a decision of great importance must be made. He feels a kinship with the shifting, changing sands and the sheer vastness of the space. Returning to the desert is a return to his heritage, and as late as 1973, his parents still lived in a goatskin tent near Sidra. Their son still prefers simple surroundings to pomp and splendor.

A second important influence on the young Qaddafi was the Islamic religion. The Qaddafis were devout Moslems and taught their son to live by the strict rules of Islamic law: no gambling, no alcoholic drinks, no promiscuity. Qaddafi still lives the austere life of a devout Moslem and is intolerant of anyone who lives differently.

Young Muammar was also influenced by the tradition of storytelling, which is a favorite pastime of Bedouin elders. In the evenings, when the chores are done and the children lie sleepily around the fire, the elders of the tribe begin to tell their stories. The stories young Muammar el-Qaddafi heard were not myths, legends, fairy tales, or ghost stories but tales about the

Qaddafi family's struggle against the Italian colonialists. Italy's invasion of Libya in 1911 and its subsequent victory took precedence over everything else in the minds of the Qaddafis. Muammar's father and uncle had been imprisoned for resisting the Italian colonial authorities; one of his grandfathers had died during the Italian invasion. As a child, Muammar was constantly reminded that his country was not free, and he was very young when he decided that when he grew up he would fight to win freedom for Libya.

Qaddafi was ten years old when Gamal Abdel Nasser staged a coup and overthrew King Farouk of Egypt in 1952. Nasser intended to make Egypt a power in the Middle East. He was a firm believer in Arab nationalism and denounced Israel and its chief ally, the United States. Nasser broadcast his views frequently on "Voice of the Arabs," a Cairo radio station to which Qaddafi listened faithfully. Qaddafi thought Nasser was the savior of his people and of the Arab world, and he wanted to be like him when he was older.

Qaddafi's father was determined that his son would receive a good education, and he saved every penny he could to send the boy to the Islamic School in Sidra. School work came easily to Muammar and he skipped several grades. After graduating from elementary school, he entered secondary school and began the activism that would characterize his later life. While other boys played games, Muammar, inspired by his idol, Nasser, led anti-Israeli demonstrations. By 1959 he had founded a secret society that plotted to overthrow King Idris of Libya, whom Qaddafi despised for being weak. Libya was independent now, Italy having lost its colonial rights after World War II, but King Idris had allowed the United States and Great Britain to build military bases in Libya in return for financial subsidies. To Qaddafi's mind that was hardly true independence.

Qaddafi attended the University of Libya, and after graduation in 1963, he enrolled in the Libyan Military Academy in Benghazi. His fellow cadets were impressed by his powers of persuasion, and he soon formed another secret society. Its members vowed to work for Libya's independence and to follow the rigid rules of the Koran.

Qaddafi graduated from military school in 1965 with an army commission. The following year, he went to England for six months of advanced training in armored warfare. He found England damp, cold, and dreary and could not wait to get home to the desert. Over the next few years, he rose steadily in the ranks of the Libyan Army, and by August 1969 he had attained the rank of captain in the Libyan Signal Corps.

Meanwhile, he and his Center Committee, the secret society he had formed at the military academy, continued to plot to gain control of the government, so that they might lead Libya to a place of power in the Arab world. They had studied the police and internal security forces of their country and decided that they presented no real threat to their plans. In fact, many members of the seven-thousand-man army were easily recruited by Qaddafi's group.

By March 1969, all was ready for the coup, but Qaddafi wanted to be certain of victory, and at the last minute he postponed action in favor of more preparation. In August the revolutionaries learned of a plot against Crown Prince Hassan al-Rida, King Idris's nephew, in the eastern region of Cyrenaica. It seemed to Qaddafi that he and his group should take advantage of the obvious unrest in the country. On September 1, 1969, he gave the signal to go ahead, and the coup took place. He divided his forces, which were headed by Signal Corps officers, and directed that several units descend simultaneously on Tripoli and Benghazi. His men took control of the royal palaces, government offices, and communication centers without a shot being fired, and thereafter their revolution was called "The Bloodless Coup."

Qaddafi, not yet thirty years old, had fulfilled his childhood dream: Libya was free of foreign influence. He went to work immediately to take full control of the government. He dissolved the Libyan parliament and other constitutional bodies and replaced them with a twelve-member Revolutionary Command Council. The Council renamed the country the Libyan Arab Republic and adopted as their national slogan "Socialism, Unity, and Freedom." Qaddafi assumed the rank of colonel and the position of Commander in Chief of the Libyan Armed Forces.

In their first statement to the world, the Revolutionary Command Council pledged to build Libya into a socialist country; to combat racism, colonialism, and social oppression; and to adhere to the spiritual precepts of the Koran. At the same time, it assured foreigners that existing trade agreements would be respected and that their lives and property would be safeguarded. Many western governments were relieved to hear this, for they depended on Libya's oil. The United States extended recognition to the new regime immediately—on September 6th—and the following day, King Idris, who had been traveling in Greece and Turkey, sent word that he was willing to abdicate. (King Idris died in Egypt in May 1983.)

Using Nasser's Arab socialism as a model, Qaddafi promoted public works projects, increased minimum-wage rates, and dismissed hundreds of corrupt government officials. To bring about the "Arabization" of the country, the Revolutionary Command Council decreed that the teaching of English in public school was to be discontinued and that all signs, posters, and public notices were to be written in Arabic. In strict conformity to Koranic doctrine, alcoholic beverages were banned, and nightclubs, brothels, and gambling casinos were closed. By November 1969 the new government had nationalized—taken over—all foreign banks. By December Qaddafi had begun to take steps to implement his dream of Arab dominance in the Middle East. That month, in Tripoli, he met with his childhood idol, Gamal Abdel Nasser, and Gaafar al-Nimeiry of the Sudan to map out a unified strategy against Israel.

Almost immediately, however, he had to turn his attention back to internal matters. A discontented faction within the new regime challenged the power of the Revolutionary Command Council. Qaddafi reorganized the government, taking over the positions of premier and minister of defense. Included in his new twelve-member cabinet were four members of the original Revolutionary Command Council and his second-in-command, Major Abdul Salam Jalloud.

Next Qaddafi turned his attention to other potential sources of unrest in the country—namely, the foreign presence. He spoke out against the British and American military bases in

Libya and did all he could to make life unpleasant for the troops stationed there. Soon the English decided to abandon their bases at Tobruk and El Adem. The Americans left Wheelus Air Base three months later. In July 1970, the Libyan government confiscated the property of Italian and Jewish residents of Libya. Most of the Jews, knowing how Qaddafi felt about Israel, had left the country immediately after the coup. The Italians, perhaps unaware of the deep bitterness Qaddafi felt toward them, had remained; that summer some twenty thousand of them were forced to leave the country. Tripoli's majestic Cathedral of the Sacred Heart of Jesus, built by the Italians, was taken over and renamed Gamal Abdel Nasser Mosque.

Despite the effects of these actions on individuals and on the military strategy of the United States and Great Britain, Qaddafi had thus far done nothing to cause alarm in the rest of the world. Many political analysts feel, in fact, that Qaddafi's flame in the Middle East would have fizzled and died out long ago if Libya were not so rich in a major world commodity—oil.

Libya is second only to Saudi Arabia in oil exports. In taking control of Libya, Qaddafi also took control of some of the largest oil fields in the world. A year after the coup, he changed his mind about not tampering with existing trade agreements. In 1970 he pressured foreign oil companies into agreeing to increases in oil prices and higher taxes. In June 1973, he announced the takeover of the Libyan branch of the Bunker Hunt Oil Company of Dallas, Texas, giving as his reason charges that Israeli spies had been allowed to enter the country through the company. In July he ordered an immediate government takeover of the remaining American oil holdings in Libya. Argued out of that idea by the oil companies, and realizing that he did not have the personnel to run them, he ordered the nationalization of only fifty-one percent of the companies' assets. Although only partially successful, Qaddafi's confrontation with the Western oil companies brought him considerable prestige in the Arab world.

Qaddafi wanted that prestige. He wanted very much to be like Nasser of Egypt and to act as the leading advocate of Arab unity. In 1971 Libya, Egypt, and Syria joined together to form a loose alliance called the Federation of Arab Republics. Under this arrangement, the three countries agreed to act as one in their trade and foreign policies. Over the next two years, Qaddafi pressured Egypt to join with Libya to form a unified state, but Egypt, under Anwar el-Sadat, chose not to go along with the plan. In Sadat's opinion, Qaddafi's rigid standards— which left no room for tolerance—and his radical behavior were not the ingredients for cooperation. The countries remained loosely connected under the Federation of Arab Republics, but they drew no closer. Qaddafi blamed Sadat for the failure of the merger, but his own acts caused many Arab leaders to be leery of him.

Qaddafi's primary interests seemed to lie in terrorism and international meddling. In 1970, when King Hussein of Jordan was fighting to keep the PLO from overthrowing his government, Qaddafi sent Yasir Arafat three hundred men to help him win the battle; relations between Hussein and Qaddafi have been strained ever since.

In 1971 he openly supported a coup against King Hassan II of Morocco. He called for an Islamic holy war against India for its role in the India-Pakistan conflict. He helped to stop a pro-Communist officer from seizing power in the Sudan. He encouraged Malta's leftist prime minister, Dominic Mintoff, to demand the withdrawal of North Atlantic Treaty Organization (NATO) troops and the evacuation of British naval forces and to reject offers of help from the Soviet Union.

When Palestinian terrorists massacred eleven Israeli athletes at the 1972 Olympic Games in Munich, Qaddafi staged a heroes' welcome for the assassins who managed to escape.

In 1973 Qaddafi sent Libyan troops across the country's southern border into Chad, a nation that had suffered constant internal conflict since gaining its independence from France thirteen years earlier. Under the guise of helping one of the two warring factions in Chad, Qaddafi's forces annexed the Aozou Strip, a mineral-rich desert area near the Chad-Libya border.

Among the minerals of the Aozou Strip was uranium, a necessary ingredient in the manufacture of nuclear weapons. Qaddafi made no secret of his desire for such weapons. It is said

that he offered the Chinese a fortune to help him develop them—
and that they refused. For a time, he worked with Pakistan on
the joint development of a nuclear bomb, but the partnership
dissolved because of disagreements. At present there are approximately seventy Arab scientists working in Libya's atomic
weapons program.

Qaddafi also sent large contributions to the Irish Republican
Army in Northern Ireland and to black militant groups in the
United States. He persuaded his friend Idi Amin, the president
of Uganda, to expel Israeli technicians and adopt an anti-Israeli
position.

During the middle and late 1970's, Qaddafi seemed to direct
more of his attention to his own country. He built an impressive
arsenal of conventional weapons, using oil revenues to buy
sophisticated arms and planes from the Soviet Union. He did not
pay equal attention to developing the personnel to use them,
however. Even today, the Libyan Army—fifty-three thousand
strong—is among the best equipped and most poorly trained in
the world. Tanks rust in the desert sands because there is no one
to drive them. Qaddafi has brought more than two thousand
Soviet-bloc military advisers to improve the competence of his
forces.

Qaddafi has spent his country's oil money on more than
armaments. He has also built roads, communications systems,
housing, parks, and schools. In the fourteen years of his dictatorship, Libya has been transformed into the world's fifteenth richest country, and the overall standard of living in Libya is much
better than it was before he came to power. In contrast to his
stated program of 1969, however, the people enjoy less freedom.

Qaddafi instituted the death penalty for illegal (by his definition) political activity and made imprisonment the automatic
penalty for strikes, worker absenteeism, and unauthorized press
releases. He reinstated the old Sharia, or Islamic law.

As part of what he called his "cultural revolution," Qaddafi
demanded a purge of "sick people"—those who supported
communism, atheism, or capitalism. He dismissed thousands of
people in business, industry, and education, jailed thousands
more, and conducted book-burnings. To replace the books he
had banned, he wrote *The Green Book*, three pocket-sized

pamphlets that explain his "Third Universal Theory"—his prescription for a new form of society that is, in his phrase, "higher" than western democracy or Soviet communism.

A major part of Qaddafi's theory of a higher form of society is his own preeminence in it, although he calls himself simply a "messenger for the people." He abolished the Libyan government and installed a variety of People's Committees to run businesses, government agencies, and communications centers. He renamed Libya the Socialist People's Libyan Arab Jamahiriya (Jamahiriya means "State of the Masses"). "The people decide everything," one Libyan reported, "but it is the thoughts of Brother Qaddafi which guide us on the proper path."

Qaddafi dropped all his other titles and asked to be known only as Brother Colonel. No matter what his title or how many People's Committees there were, Brother Colonel ran the country, and he was accountable to no one.

At that time, the Libyan people did not seem to mind, for Qaddafi had built a generous welfare state in which every citizen was guaranteed food, housing, and clothing. They were reminded of his benevolence by the portraits of him that seemed to be everywhere. In these portraits, he was almost always pictured alone, although in some he was shown with Gamal Abdel Nasser. On balance, Qaddafi was extremely successful with his domestic policies. He wanted to be successful in the world arena as well, however. By the late 1970's he began to show that he was as unpredictable as ever—and as bent on fomenting trouble as he had been a few years earlier.

In 1979 he airlifted two thousand Libyans to Uganda in an unsuccessful effort to shore up the repressive regime of Idi Amin. In the same year, he sent a howling mob to wreck the United States Embassy in Tripoli to show his support for Iran's Ayatollah Khomeini. And he became the most outspoken critic of the Camp David accords, for in his vision of the Middle East there was no room for Israel. "Israel," he cried, "must be destroyed!" He was equally convinced that Arab moderates and pro-Western leaders in the Middle East—like Anwar el-Sadat—had to be overthrown. With eyes flashing, he proclaimed proudly that he was not afraid to "declare war on the United States" if necessary.

In April 1981 the United States Sixth Fleet was on maneuvers in the south central Mediterranean Sea. French aircraft had been harassed over the Mediterranean by Libyan planes, and the American naval pilots had been warned to be ready for trouble. One morning, two F-14's from the aircraft carrier *Nimitz* swung south, spotted a blip on their radar, and moved to identify it. The blip was a Libyan Su-22 fighter. As the American fighters approached, the pilot of the Libyan Su-22 fired and missed. The Americans fired back and scored a hit. As the Libyan pilot parachuted to safety, the Su-22 went down.

At first the incident threatened to assume major proportions. Charges were made on both sides. The problem was Qaddafi's interpretation of maritime law. Most countries claim only three miles of ocean as their territorial waters, but Qaddafi has always claimed twelve. The United States refused to recognize his claim and insisted that the F-14's were over international waters when attacked, therefore, they had had every right to fight back. Qaddafi got little support from the rest of the world for his claim of sovereignty over waters beyond the three-mile limit, and the furor over the incident subsided. There has been little or no talk about war with the United States in Libya since.

Meanwhile, in 1980, Qaddafi had launched an invasion into Chad, sending eight thousand soldiers with Soviet-made tanks and jets to back one of the warring factions. At one time or another between 1978 and 1983, his extremist views managed to alienate the governments of both Saudi Arabia and Iraq and of fourteen African states. Anwar el-Sadat called him a "goon" and a "madman." Another neighbor and head of state, Gaafar al-Nimeiry of the Sudan, said that Qaddafi had a split personality and that both parts were evil. Even some factions of the radical PLO began to tire of his refusal to consider negotiations of any kind with the Israelis.

Regarded with suspicion by most other Arab leaders, Qaddafi realized that his dream of leading a powerful union of Arab states was in serious jeopardy. More than that, he was in danger of being isolated in the Middle East. Accordingly, he took steps to heal the rifts between himself and the other Arab leaders. On January 1, 1982, Saudi Arabia and Libya resumed diplomatic relations, after a fourteen month break occasioned by Qaddafi's vehement opposition (which he still maintains) to the Fahd Plan for peace with Israel. Iraq and Libya also resumed normal relations. President Hosni Mubarak asked Egyptian news reporters to stop calling Qaddafi names, and the borders between Libya and Egypt, closed since the signing of the Camp David accords, were reopened in 1982.

Qaddafi did not end his efforts to become a major influence among African nations. Geographically, Libya is an African country, and Qaddafi has long wanted to be a powerful spokesman for the countries to the south of Libya. He tried for several years to court the members of the Organization of African Unity and was rebuffed; but he kept on trying. The OAU held its nineteenth annual four-day summit meeting in August 1982, and Qaddafi very much wanted to become chairman of the organization, for the position would give him credibility and recognition. In order to guarantee that he would be elected, he used every bit of influence he had to try to arrange to have the meeting held in Libya. However, not enough African leaders showed up to allow a vote to be taken. Angrily, Qaddafi accused the United States of somehow fixing things so that he could not get his way.

The following year, in June 1983, he was again denied the chairmanship of the OAU. Furthermore, the OAU members present at the conference barred the groups he backed in Chad and western Sahara from participating in the meeting.

Within hours of his OAU defeat, Qaddafi embarked upon a tour of Arab capitals in an attempt to shore up his relations with the Middle Eastern countries. He visited King Fahd in Saudi Arabia, King Hussein in Jordan, and King Hassan in Morocco. He visited Syria and Yemen and even tried to arrange a meeting with PLO leader Yasir Arafat. Arafat would not meet with Qaddafi and accused him of giving support to the rebellious factions within the PLO. Despite the rejection by Arafat, Qaddafi seemed to have become more willing to compromise on the subject of Israel. From his discussions with other Arab leaders, he had begun to understand that the emphasis in relations with Israel was now more on negotiation than on confrontation and that to regain the confidence of the other leaders, he would have to moderate, or appear to moderate, his opinions.

He did not, however, take a more moderate stance in his policy toward Chad. In August 1983, Libyan troops invaded Chad yet a third time, causing both France and the United States to consider sending forces to aid the opposing side in the ongoing civil war. Once France had committed itself to send aid, the United States held back—perhaps because it wanted to maintain its trade arrangements with Libya.

Despite public posturing, the United States and Libya continue to do business. Qaddafi still regards the West as corrupt, and the United States still regards Qaddafi as a madman. America's Libyan Embassy remains closed, but in 1981 the United States bought thirty-eight percent of Libya's oil, and that figure has remained approximately the same in subsequent years. (In 1983 Qaddafi tried to buy an American system for moving and loading oil tankers offshore; he was turned down.) Among the eight hundred thousand foreigners who work in oil-related industries in Libya are many Americans; they report that life there is not as difficult as they had expected it to be.

They also report, however, that Qaddafi is not as popular among his own people as he used to be. Declining oil prices have made it necessary for him to cut back on some domestic programs. Libyans are unhappy about his repressive policies and about the loss of life resulting from his various foreign adventures. There have been assassination plots in his own country, and according to unofficial reports, he was shot in the jaw in late 1982. He disappeared from public view for several weeks, and when he emerged he was accompanied by squads of bodyguards. At first the guards were East Germans—and primarily men. By June 1983 his protectors included a large number of women, some of them in high heels.

It is clear that a major part of Muammar el-Qaddafi's dream has been frustrated. He has not managed to become a major world leader. He is feared, not admired. He has not succeeded in leading the Arab states to the union that he has long envisioned; nor has he managed to gain control of the federation of African leaders to the south. He faces unrest in his own country. If he is going to hold on to even parts of his dream, he is going to have to do something new, and soon; but no one knows what he might do.

Qaddafi remains a mystery. Alone and in the company of people he trusts, he does not seem like a lunatic. He has not used Libya's oil billions to enhance his own standard of living. He has not surrounded himself with the trappings of wealth. He prefers to wear ancestral robes and his military uniform, although he will put on a suit and tie when the occasion calls for them. He prefers to work out of a tent rather than a luxurious suite of offices. He can speak English well, but often uses an Arabic dialect when interviewed by Western reporters, thus enjoying the advantage of being able to understand without being understood. Qaddafi often travels around his country in disguise, learning firsthand the feelings of the people. He never misses the daily prayers prescribed by the Koran.

His marriage to a teacher named Fathia Nouri Khaled in 1969 quickly ended in divorce, and he married again a year later. His present wife is Wasfia, a nurse. He has two sons, Mohammed by his first wife, and Seif el-Islam, by his second. Although he is very attractive physically—news cameramen from all over the world like to be assigned to cover him—there is nothing especially noteworthy about his manner or bearing, nothing to indicate the radical actions he is inclined to take. He walks about with his hands in his pockets and seems, on first contact, to be very shy. As one journalist wrote, "It is only in his eyes that one can sense the fanatic."

11

MOHAMMAD

ZIA

UL-HAQ

Pakistan

Mohammad Zia ul-Haq

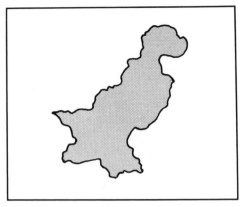

Pakistan

11

General Mohammad Zia ul-Haq is the chief of state of the Islamic Republic of Pakistan, a country that is located in southern Asia and that is not geographically in the Middle East. Pakistan is generally considered a Middle Eastern country, however, because ninety percent of its people are Moslems, the main religion in every other country in the Middle East except Israel. On the west, Pakistan borders Iran, and there is an important Shiite Moslem community in Pakistan. On balance, the people of Pakistan consider themselves more akin to the Arab Middle East than to their neighbors on the north (the Soviet Union), to the east (China), and to the south and east (India). They are especially adamant about not being linked with India, from which they separated in 1947.

Until the eighth century, the people on the Indian subcontinent were primarily Hindus, who followed an ancient faith that had developed over a period of about four thousand years. During the eighth century, Moslem Arabs, bent on spreading the influence of Islam, conquered the northwestern Indian province of Sind. Moslems failed to make further headway in India until about 1000 A.D., when another period of expansion culminated in the establishment of the Mogul Empire (1526-1857). During much of this time, the Moslems and the Hindus on the Indian subcontinent lived in relative harmony, but their differences were never far below the surface. The Hindu Mahrattas rose to power in India in the 17th century and held sway until the British subdued them in 1818.

Beginning in the late 1830's, the British government gained control of most of the Indian subcontinent. Under British rule rifts between the Moslems and Hindus began to resurface. The more educated and affluent Indians, most of whom were Hindus, adopted English ways and learned the English language. In return, the British favored them and gave them more influence in the government. Before long, the Hindus were the privileged class.

The Moslems, on the other hand, refused to abandon their customs and held fast to their traditions. Their social and economic status in India diminished, and they had little voice in running the country.

Both religious groups wanted India to be independent of Great Britain. The Hindus were chafing under British rule. And the Moslems, fearing that the Hindu majority would work toward independence without taking them into account, founded the All-India Moslem League in 1906. Its purpose was the promotion of Moslem rights. As far as independence was concerned, however, the British had no intention of giving up their colony of India, and it was many years before India became an independent state.

When Mohammad Zia ul-Haq was born in 1924, in the northern province of Punjab, he was born into a British-dominated country. His parents were Moslems, but unlike many other Moslems in India, they were of the middle class and could afford to give their son an education based on the principles and teachings of the Moslem holy book, the Koran.

Zia's parents did not oppose the British rule; they sent their son to British schools and apparently encouraged—or at least did not discourage—his dream of becoming a soldier in the British tradition. As a boy, Zia saw and was deeply impressed by a poster of a British soldier, and he decided to become just like that image—military, suave, and dignified.

Zia attended St. Stephen's College in Delhi. He then enrolled in the Royal Indian Military Academy at Dehra Dun in the Himalayan foothills. He received his military commission in May 1945 and served in the last months of World War II with a British armored division in Southeast Asia.

The end of World War II brought a major change in the politics of India. Great Britain was ready to relinquish control and wanted to leave behind a region that would be stable and friendly. Indian Moslems had continued, during all this time, to press their own interests, as distinct from those of the Hindu majority. In 1930 a Moslem-Indian poet, Sir Mohammed Iqbal, had proposed that India be separated into two states, one Hindu and one Moslem. The Moslem League had supported that idea and promoted it. Eventually, the Moslem League persuaded the British that such a division would be the best way to guarantee the safety and stability of the region.

In 1947, under the provisions of the Indian Independence Act, Britain reluctantly agreed to the formation of a separate Moslem state—Pakistan, Land of the Pure. Created for religious rather than geographical reasons, Pakistan consisted of two regions—East Bengal (later East Pakistan) and West Pakistan— that were separated by more than one thousand miles.

The whole transfer of power was badly organized and rife with turmoil. While India was able to assume the administrative machinery left behind by the British, Pakistan began with practically nothing. Records had to be transferred from Delhi, India's capital, to a makeshift capital for Pakistan at Karachi. Everywhere, it seemed, Hindus and Moslems were fighting each other, for the division meant the uprooting of thousands. The rioting and panic took more than a million lives as Moslems and Hindus fled to their own lands. More than seven million Moslems fled to Pakistan from India, and ten million Hindus left Pakistan for India. The fear and enmity of pre- and post-partition days have not yet subsided and continue to influence the politics of the Indian subcontinent.

Immediately after independence, India and Pakistan became involved in a dispute over boundaries: both claimed the northern Indian province of Kashmir. While the majority of people there were Moslems, the government was Hindu. Indian and Pakistani troops clashed in the small, mountainous region, and for years Kashmir remained a divided territory, half in India, half in Pakistan.

Mohammad Zia ul-Haq did not see any action in these border wars. When the British left the newly-created state of Pakistan in 1947, officers of his caliber were appointed to top positions in the new Pakistani Army. Mohammed Ali Jinnah, the first Governor-General of Pakistan—also called the Father of the Pakistan Nation—believed that his armed forces needed much training. Zia was assigned to instruct army recruits.

It appeared for a while as though Zia was going to spend his career as a mere instructor. Not until the 1950's, when he was close to thirty years old, was he sent to the Staff College at Quetta; there his work finally brought him notice. In 1959, after graduation, he was sent to the United States to take advanced military training at the Command and General Staff College at Fort Leavenworth, Kansas. Within a year of his return to Pakistan, he took a teaching position at the Staff College at Quetta.

While teaching at his old school, Zia distinguished himself as a military theoretician, but he longed to have an opportunity to put his ideas into action. In 1965 he got that opportunity and took a command in Kashmir, where Indian and Pakistani troops still clashed over boundaries and the control of water-power resources. All-out warfare in Kashmir lasted only a couple of months. The Soviet Union, which was worried about the constant fighting in an area so near its southern border, hosted talks between the president of Pakistan and the prime minister of India that resulted in the signing of a peace treaty at Tashkent, in the Soviet Union, in 1966. While the treaty did not solve the basic conflict over Kashmir, it did bring an end to the fighting, and Lieutenant Colonel Zia left Kashmir. He remained on active duty, however. He was given command of a cavalry regiment and in May 1968 was promoted to full colonel and assigned to an armored division.

By 1969, the Palestine Liberation Organization presence in Jordan had become so strong that King Hussein was concerned about his ability to control them. He approached Pakistan's President Ayub Khan for help; Ayub agreed to provide military advisers. Colonel Zia was among the Pakistani officers sent to Jordan, where he served from 1969 to 1971. For his aid to the Jordanian Army, which moved against the PLO in September 1970 and succeeded in ousting them from Jordan by July 1971, he was awarded two medals by the Jordanian government.

Back home in Pakistan, the forty-two-year-old professional soldier was promoted to brigadier general and given command of another armored brigade. He was soon back in action.

East Pakistan had been plagued by unrest since independence in 1947. Then called East Bengal, it was a thousand miles from West Pakistan, the center of government. Not until the 1950's was it renamed East Pakistan, and not until 1962 did a new constitution provide for a federal Islamic republic with two provinces (East and West Pakistan) and two official languages (Bengali and Urdu). Over the next decade, the people of East Pakistan were often discontented with the government of West Pakistan, and there was a rising sentiment for independence. On March 26, 1971, East Pakistan declared its independence as the country of Bangladesh. Troops from West Pakistan moved in immediately to put down the insurrection and occupy the region. Brigadier General Zia was among these forces.

In December 1971, India, which supported Bangladesh, sent troops into East Pakistan, and India and Pakistan went to war. The war lasted less than two weeks and ended in the defeat of Pakistan. After that, Pakistan's president, Ayub Khan, resigned and was replaced by Deputy Premier and Foreign Minister Zulfikar Ali Bhutto, who eventually granted recognition to the new nation of Bangladesh in 1974. During this time, Zia served in East Pakistan-Bangladesh as a deputy armored division commander.

With each military action, Zia rose a step in the ranks of the Pakistani Army. In 1975 he was promoted to lieutenant general and made a corps commander. The following year he advanced to the rank of general and became Army Chief of Staff. Until this time, Zia had not been interested in politics. He had dedicated his life to soldiering and had concentrated his efforts on advancing his military career. That is precisely why Prime Minister Ali Bhutto picked him for such a high post.

Army Chief of Staff is a powerful position, and a man with political ambitions might be tempted to use it to gain influence in the government. Because Zia lacked such ambition, Bhutto was confident that he would not be an obstacle to his populist rule. Other observers agreed with Bhutto. Zia's reputation as a religious leader was mediocre at best, and his loyalty to Bhutto caused people to call him "Bhutto's butler." All those people—Bhutto included—underestimated Zia. He turned out to be a political force to be reckoned with, and in later years some people suggested that Zia had deliberately played the role of a stooge in order to secure his position.

At the time Bhutto appointed Zia Army Chief of Staff, the Pakistani people were growing increasingly restless. Pakistan had been engaged in fighting on one front or another for years, and in directing most of the country's resources toward the military, Pakistan's leaders had neglected domestic needs. Bhutto had also departed from many Islamic traditions, and religious leaders were against him. Bhutto had also promised more freedom, but the people had seen little evidence of the greater democracy he had assured them they would enjoy under his regime. A variety of factions challenged him to keep his promises, and, accordingly, he promised free elections in early 1977.

Nine political parties united to form the Pakistan National Alliance (PNA) to oppose Bhutto in the elections on March 7, and when Bhutto's Pakistan People's party (PPP) took 155 of the 200 National Assembly seats, the PNA charged that he had rigged the elections. That summer there were violent protests across the country. The protesters called for new—and really free—elections and for the resignation of the Bhutto government.

Bhutto refused to resign, and the PNA called for a general strike. In response, Bhutto ordered the arrest of the PNA leaders and ordered his Army Chief of Staff, General Zia, to establish military rule in the major cities.

Zia reluctantly obeyed Bhutto's orders. Before taking action, he called together the various army corps commanders to discuss the best way the army could help to end the civil strife.

The consensus was that Prime Minister Bhutto ought to make a political settlement with his opponents as quickly as possible. Supposedly, Bhutto had already taken steps at reform and had called for a referendum to allow the people to decide his fate. When Zia made his report to the prime minister, he discovered that Bhutto was not serious about risking his power in a free election. Bhutto was determined to maintain his position, by force if necessary. "With your brawn and my brain," he told Zia, "we can rule the country."

Though dismayed by Bhutto's statement and secret plans, Zia at first rejected the idea of taking over the government from Bhutto by force. "We soldiers must stay above politics," he declared in May 1977. As rioting against the Bhutto administration continued, and as Bhutto steadfastly refused to negotiate with his opponents, Zia changed his mind. On July 5, 1977, Bhutto and members of his cabinet were arrested at a mountain resort where they were meeting, and in a bloodless coup the army, led by Zia, took control of the government of Pakistan.

Although Zia reassured the people that he held no personal political ambitions and was only filling the vacuum created by dishonest political leaders, his actions seemed to belie his promises. As Chief Martial Law Administrator, he immediately suspended all legislative assemblies and political parties; he also banned all trade union activity and political activism. He re-instituted the Islamic legal codes. Such measures were supposed to be temporary, until the civil strife in Pakistan ended and free elections, called for the following October, gave the Pakistani people the opportunity to choose their own leaders and their own legal codes. Zia chose not to use Islamic law to punish former Prime Minister Bhutto, as Pakistan's religious leaders urged, saying, "Let us not be emotional but practical." He did not feel it would benefit Pakistan in the long run to stage an emotion-filled trial that would end in the execution of the former prime minister.

Emotions against Bhutto ran high, however, at least among the people who surrounded Zia, and at length he announced that he had reviewed secret reports and memoranda from the former prime minister's files and that his investigation showed that Bhutto should be tried. This announcement created more unrest in Pakistan. During the trial there were mass demonstrations in favor of Bhutto.

There was too much unrest, in Zia's opinion, for the promised national elections to be held in October; on October 1, he announced their indefinite postponement. "There needs to be more stability. . . a period to cool off. . . [a] return to a calm atmosphere," he explained. Then he imposed even tighter martial-law restrictions and ordered more arrests.

Apparently, the nonpolitical career soldier had changed his mind. He enjoyed power and did not wish to give it up soon. Publicly, he continued to promise that free elections would be held soon. In November 1977 the Pakistani Supreme Court approved Zia's military takeover as a "doctrine of necessity," but it warned Zia to hold the promised elections as soon as possible.

They had still not been held when, on September 16, 1978, Zia was sworn in as president of the Islamic Republic of Pakistan. In his inaugural address, he promised again to step down once a successor was chosen in a national election, but he would not say when that election would be held.

Zia continued to lead his country back to the traditions of Islam. He banned all non-Islamic political parties and by February 1979 had formally introduced Koranic *Zakat* and *Ushr* laws into Pakistan's legal code. Among other things, these ancient laws provided for Pakistanis to tithe, or donate a percentage of their personal savings, investments, and farm products to the government. The money would be used to finance much-needed social welfare programs. It was under Islamic law that in 1979 former Prime Minister Bhutto was finally executed, after being held prisoner for over a year and a half.

World leaders appealed to Zia to show mercy. After the Pakistani Supreme Court upheld Bhutto's conviction for murder by a four-to-three vote, President Jimmy Carter of the United States sent Zia a personal letter asking him to commute the sentence. Leonid Brezhnev of the Soviet Union and heads of state throughout the Moslem world also asked Zia to grant clemency to Bhutto. Zia refused to pardon his predecessor; Bhutto was hanged on April 4, 1979.

Nationwide protests followed the execution, and many of the protesters cried for Zia's death. In response, Zia set a new date for national elections—November 17, 1979—but after Bhutto's daughter Benazir, whose mother leads the Pakistan People's party, charged that Zia would rig the elections, he cancelled them again.

There followed another wave of arrests, and political activity was again banned. The country, Zia declared, was too unstable for elections to be held. Besides, he added offhandedly, there were more pressing matters that needed his attention. Among these was the establishment of a strict Islamic regime. In pursuit of that goal, Zia outlawed all strikes and prohibited the publication of newspapers and magazines that "poisoned and polluted" Pakistani minds. It is probably no coincidence that in the same month that Zia once again cancelled free elections in Pakistan, Islamic fundamentalist revolutionaries in Iran seized the United States embassy in Teheran and took sixty-two Americans hostage. It is certainly worth mentioning that by this time Iran's Ayatollah Ruhollah Khomeini had also ordered press censorship.

Zia felt the power and rage of extreme Islamic fundamentalism when in November 1979 the United States embassy in Islamabad was burned by Moslem militants who mistakenly thought the United States had been involved in the takeover of the Grand Mosque in Mecca. Zia hastened to assure the United States that he had known nothing of the plot. Although he is committed to a return to Islamic traditions, Zia is not an extremist like Khomeini, and, in fact, he tried to use his status as a strong supporter of Islamic fundamentalism to persuade the Ayatollah to release the American hostages. He does not, however, want to alienate Moslem fundamentalists in Pakistan.

Zia is also a pragmatist when it comes to international relations. That means that he bases his foreign-policy decisions not so much on emotionalism or religious fundamentalism as on an assessment of what he thinks Pakistan needs. He does not want Pakistan to be dominated by any other country, and thus he makes and breaks alliances without following any set philosophy.

As chairman of the Islamic Conference, Zia visited Teheran and Baghdad in September 1980 in an effort to bring to an end the war between Iran and Iraq. In October of that year he spoke to the United Nations General Assembly and called for a negotiated solution to that long and bloody war. He has maintained close relations with other Islamic countries (which is how he was elected chairman of the Islamic Conference). Upon the death of King Khalid in 1982, he visited Saudi Arabia to pay his condolences.

Zia has not sought an alliance with the Soviet Union, although in 1982 he attended the funeral of Leonid Brezhnev in Moscow. In the main, he seems to be suspicious of his northern neighbor. He angrily denounced the Russians in December 1979, when they invaded Afghanistan, and he allowed Afghanistani refugees to enter his country. When, in 1981, the Russians violated Pakistani airspace and frontiers, he appealed to the United States for military support.

By then Ronald Reagan was President of the United States, and his administration continued the overtures to Pakistan begun by Carter. Carter had opposed the execution of former Prime Minister Bhutto and worried about Pakistan's nuclear program, begun by Bhutto and continued by Zia. But after the Soviet invasion of Afghanistan, he had offered military aid to Zia. The Reagan Administration wanted to reward Zia for accepting Afghanistani refugees and offered new military and economic aid to Pakistan.

For his part, Zia wanted to maintain his nonaligned status, and though he welcomed the economic aid, he chose to pay for the arms. On September 15, 1981, the Pakistani and American governments announced a $3.2-billion package of economic aid and military sales for a six-year period.

Zia's standing with other leaders, and with the rest of the world, depends greatly on the stability of Pakistan. The more unrest there is in his country, the weaker is his voice in international affairs. Viewed from a Western perspective, the fact that he has continued to exercise martial law and has not held free elections makes him a ruler of questionable stability, especially because popular unrest in Pakistan continues.

It might be argued that Zia is not the only nondemocratic ruler in the Middle East who says he is committed to eventual democratic rule. King Hussein was supposed to have stepped down long ago to allow Jordan to move from a monarchy to a democracy. He has not done so, nor does he intend to, but, for the time being, Jordan does not suffer from political unrest the way Pakistan does. Pakistan has known little else since its founding, and by the latter part of 1983, Zia's rule was causing renewed turmoil.

The trouble began in August in Sind, Ali Bhutto's home province. Nonviolent protests against the Zia government did not remain centered there, however, but spread to other Pakistani cities. Led by the Movement for the Restoration of Democracy—a coalition of eight banned political parties—the protesters demanded an immediate end to military rule, free elections, and the restoration of constitutional government. The government countered by sending troops to put down the protests. By November, several villages had been destroyed, at least two hundred people had been shot dead, some twenty-three thousand had been jailed, and nearly one hundred protesters had been publicly flogged. Zia continued to believe that his armed forces could put down any insurrection. He also promised that free national elections would be held in March 1985 and that at the same time martial law would be lifted and civil rights restored. Few Pakistanis could be blamed, however, for being suspicious of his promises of free elections.

Not much is known about Zia as a private man. He has kept his wife, Begum Shafia Zia, out of the spotlight. Zia has five children. His eldest son studied in the United States and works for a bank in Bahrain; his two other sons studied medicine. His older daughter is married and lives in London. His younger daughter, Zain, has a congenital heart disease and lives at home. Because of her ailment, she cannot lead an active life, and her father spends as much time with her as his schedule will allow.

Although he has been out of active military service for more than a decade, the 5'6", stockily-built Zia has kept his British military bearing. He parts his hair in the middle and sports the kind of thick mustache that distinguished British soldiers in India earlier in this century. He keeps his boots highly polished and moves with a head-up, shoulders-back stride. He departs from the image of the British soldier in many ways, however.

He begins and ends each day with prayers and has made the obligatory Moslem pilgrimage to Mecca. He lives in a modest home in Rawalpindi and rejects the more elaborate presidential residences. He does not smoke, drink, or gamble.

Wrote Gordon Brook-Shepherd of the *London Sunday Telegraph*, "It is on his orders that no pictures of him [Zia] are displayed anywhere—such a refreshing change from those Third World countries where the features of some tinpot tyrant leer at you from every office, shop, hotel lobby and airport." Indeed, Zia does not seem to be interested in the same kind of personality cult that other dictators have required.

Still, he maintains the role of dictator in other ways. He has yet to hold free elections. Until he does, he remains suspect in the eyes of the world as a man who may be confusing the interests of his country with his own interests. And based on the continuing unrest in Pakistan, he may regret that confusion, as may the rest of the world. Writing on the Op-Ed page in *The New York Times* in November 1983, a Pakistani named Eqbal Ahmad pointed out that the nonviolent demonstrations in Pakistan, having accomplished nothing, could easily escalate into violence, and that violence in a country as strategic as Pakistan—both geographically and politically—could have major repercussions. "Here," wrote Ahmad, "lie the small fuses of disputed borders and ethnic divisions that historically have ignited great wars."

Further Reading

~~~~~~

BOOKS

Baker, P. Randall. *King Hussein and the Kingdom of Hejaz.* New York: Oleander Press, 1979.

Beling, Willard A. *King Faisal and the Modernization of Saudi Arabia.* Boulder, Colo.: Westview Press, 1979.

Black, Lionel. *Arafat is Next!* Briarcliff Manor, N.Y.: Stein & Day, 1975.

Gervasi, Frank Henry. *The Life and Times of Menachem Begin.* New York: G.P. Putnam's Sons, 1979.

Kiernan, Thomas. *Arafat: The Man and the Myth.* New York: W.W. Norton, 1976.

Kissinger, Henry. *Years of Upheaval.* Boston: Little, Brown, & Co., 1982.

Lacey, Robert. *The Kingdom: Arabia and the House of Saud.* New York: Harcourt, Brace, Jovanovich, 1981.

Lacouture, Jean. *Nasser: A Biography.* New York: Alfred A. Knopf, 1973.

Malgo, William. *Begin With Sadat.* Columbia, S.C.: Midnight Collection, n.d.

Mann, C. Stephen. *A Man For All Time.* Wilton, Conn.: Morehouse, 1971.

Narayan, B.K. *Anwar el Sadat: Man With a Mission.* New York: International Publishers Service, 1976.

Polk, William R. *The Arab World.* Cambridge, Mass.: Harvard University Press, 1980.

Stone, Julius. *Israel and Palestine: Assault on the Law of Nations.* Baltimore: Johns Hopkins University Press, 1981.

Vatikiotis, P.J. *The History of Egypt From Muhammed Ali to Sadat.* Baltimore: Johns Hopkins University Press, 1980.

PERIODICALS

Current Biography
Foreign Affairs
International Who's Who
Newsweek
New York Magazine
The New York Times
Time
Who's Who in the Arab World

Index